300 GAMES
FOR ALL
OCCASIONS
compiled by
Patrick Goodland

SCRIPTURE UNION
130 City Road
London EC1V 2NJ

© Patrick Goodland 1979
First Published 1979
Fifth Reprint 1985

Much of the material included in this edition was first published
in *Games Galore* (Scripture Union, 1968).

ISBN 0 85421 678 2

Printed by R. J. Acford Chichester

DON'T START THE FIRST GAME
until you have read this . . .

Games are for physical relaxation and real enjoyment. They help us to share fun and to make friends, and are often a means of breaking down reserve and shyness.

We have prepared this book as a practical handbook for all who are involved in activities with boys and girls and young people. All the games in this book have been tried out with success. Many of their origins are unknown and some will be recognized as variations on well-known themes. Three games — *Hissing and Clapping, Jumbled Names* and *Kim's Game* — have been reprinted from *Let's Play Games!* by kind permission of Edinburgh House Press.

Don't embarrass them

★ A great number of the games, in various sections, can be adapted to suit the number of participants, their age group and the conditions prevailing. But when choosing games it is important to think carefully about the players and the situation. For example, some teenagers enjoy pencil and paper games but others would be embarrassed by them.

★ When leading games it is essential to understand the rules and to explain them clearly and briefly. It is often possible to begin the game and teach the rules as the game develops.

★ Rules and regulations should be upheld to the degree necessary for discipline and enjoyment. But over-enthusiastic referees can cause endless irritation and rob games of their interest.

Get your blindfolds first – and watch the weather

★ Where a game needs items of equipment, this is stated in the opening paragraph of the instructions about it and the paragraph is printed in italics. The equipment should be collected in advance. Don't, for example, ask for scarves for blindfolding in the middle of a programme. Sometimes people who can't or won't join in a game can be employed in looking after the equipment or keeping the score.

★ Timing is an important factor. So is the choice of your opening game which you may have to play when only half or a handful of the players have arrived.

★ Change games when they are successful. Don't wait until they have been played too long and interest is flagging.

★ Take an account of weather conditions. Don't allow children to stand around on cold, windy days and don't overtax them in a heatwave.

A little encouragement goes a long way

★ Adults should never monopolize a game for boys and girls, but a little encouragement for the losing team, especially in field games, can often renew enthusiasm. With larger groups, a microphone can be valuable in keeping control and making sure that the rules are clearly heard and understood.

★ Careful preparation, the sharing of responsibilities, and having a varied programme are three of the secrets of success.

CONTENTS

SECTION 1: OUTDOOR GAMES

SECTION 2: GAMES WITHOUT EQUIPMENT

SECTION 3: CHASING AND RUNNING GAMES

SECTION 4: WIDE AND HUNT GAMES

SECTION 5: SUGGESTIONS FOR SPORTS DAY

SECTION 6 (A): INDOOR GAMES FOR VERY YOUNG CHILDREN

SECTION 6 (B): FINGER PLAYS

SECTION 6 (C): ACTION AND MOVEMENT SONGS

SECTION 7: INDOOR GAMES FOR JUNIORS

8

SECTION 8: INDOOR GAMES FOR TEENAGERS

SECTION 1
OUTDOOR
GAMES

1 ADAPTED HOCKEY

You will need a shinty stick for each player and a frido ball.

Time: Variable – depending on stamina and enthusiasm of players.
Pitch: Approximately the size of a tennis court.
Numbers: Eleven is the best, but a few more or less makes no difference.
11+ age group.

Aim: To score goals.
Rules
   (1)   All players except two – one from each team – stand behind their respective lines.
   (2)   No player is allowed over team line.
   (3)   Two players run from their respective ends, and endeavour to get the ball over their opponents' line by hitting with shinty sticks.
   (4)   Opponents may stop the ball with their sticks but may not come over line.
   (5)   As soon as ball crosses line a goal is scored.

13

(6)   The two players continue until one or other scores a goal.

(7)   The players are numbered, and as the umpire rolls the ball in, after a goal is scored, he calls a number, and the two players with that number run in.

(8)   No player may lift his stick above his shoulder, or kick the ball deliberately.

2   BOX STACKING

You will need a quantity of large uniform size boxes.

Scatter the boxes over a wide area. Players are divided into two or more compatible teams. On commencement team members collect boxes into one vertical column. Opponents can attempt toppling another column throughout the duration of the game. On the concluding whistle the team with the highest vertical column is the winner.

3   BOUNCE HANDBALL

You will require a ball.

This game is a variation of Hand Football (see Section 7, number 26, page 73). The court can be marked out exactly as in the diagram on page 74 but the penalty area may be omitted if so desired. The object of the game is to score goals as before, but the ball must be bounced from player to player. The ball must pass through the goal at below knee height.

Though the ball may be caught, it must not be held for more than two seconds. A player may also run with the ball, but must bounce it continuously whilst so doing. No tackling is allowed, but if a player is in possession of the ball and is touched by the hand of an opponent, he must pass the ball immediately. No goal can be scored by a player after he has been touched. If two players catch the ball simultaneously, the ball must be thrown up between them.

Any rough play or infringement of rules must be

penalized immediately by a free throw at an un-defended goal from the centre line. All other rules may be as for Hand Football.

4 CIRCLE PASS OUT

You will need a small ball, a large rubber ball or a football.

This is a fairly advanced circular passing and inter-cepting game. Two large circles are drawn and the players arrange themselves as shown in diagram. The centre player endeavours to pass the ball to the outside players, not above shoulder height, those between the two circles trying to intercept the ball as it is thrown. The game is played for a given time, say, three or four minutes, and the score of good passes is kept. The inside team then changes places with the outside team and the game is restarted. A new centre thrower should take the place of the original one in the centre of the circle. If the numbers are particularly large, two, three, or even four centre throwers may be introduced.

5 CROCKER

You will need three stumps for wicket, a large ball and a baseball bat or rounders stick.

There are many variations and rules for this game; but the following have been among the best. The smaller the two sides the better, though they should not be under ten players each. The wicket is three stumps placed to cover one yard in width. The bowler's stump is seven or eight yards away in front and the stump to run to is seven or more yards away to the left. Use a large ball and a baseball bat. The ball must be bowled under-arm, from the stump, full toss between knee and shoulder height of the batsman. The batsman must run round the stump every time he hits the ball in front of the wicket. The bowler can bowl immediately the ball is returned to him. Thus you can be out, bowled, or lbw, if it hits you twice. If you are caught full toss (and you can be caught behind the wicket also), you are out. To speed up the game, the whole team can be out when someone is caught full toss; and first bounce can be sufficient for each member to be out. The winning team is that with the most runs after a given number of innings.

6 DANISH ROUNDERS

You will require a light football or frido ball.

The field of play is marked out as shown in the diagram.

The ball is pitched as in Circular Rounders, but instead of running all the way round the bases without stopping, the striker may stop on any base if he so desires.

Rules

(1)   As soon as the pitcher (who must stand with both feet inside his circle) receives the ball from his fielders, he shouts 'Stop' and all runners from the striking team who are not on bases, or safely in the striking area, are out and do not bat again that innings.

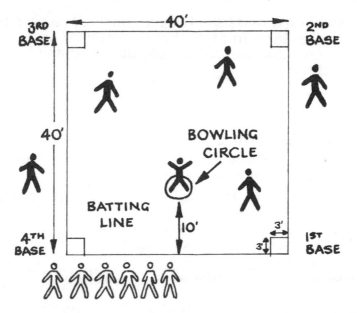

(2) The pitcher may leave his circle to field a ball, but he must not shout 'Stop' until he has both feet inside the circle again.

(3) If a runner succeeds in reaching base 4, either with or without stops at bases en route, he scores one point for his team and can strike again.

(4) If the ball is caught from a hit by the striker, both he and all the runners outside the bases are out.

(5) On striking, the striker must run for the first base, but after that he need only run for another base when the opportunity arises. Any number of players may be on the same base at any one time.

(6) If no player on the striking side is ready to bat, i.e. if they are all out or on bases, the whole side is out.

(7) If a player is successful in running round the three bases and back to home (base 4) without having to stop en route, two points are scored.

When first played, it may be necessary to adjust the distances between bases to suit local conditions and the age of the players. Outdoors, if equipment is available, a rounders or baseball bat may be used by the striker instead of the hand. In such a case, the distance between bases could be lengthened considerably.

7 DODGE BALL

You will require two or more balls, depending on age, skill and number of children.

Aim: To dismiss as many of the opposing team as possible, within a given time.

Time: This also can vary depending on numbers. Usually each game takes approximately ten to fifteen minutes, but it is one which can be repeated several times the same afternoon without palling.

Numbers: About fifteen on each side is ideal, but in a slightly longer area with more balls, greater numbers are possible.

Rules

(1) Players have allocated areas, indicated by rope or chalk lines, depending on whether played outside or inside. They must not go outside these areas.

(2) Two players from each team stand in tramlines behind the opposing team (see diagram).

(3) Two balls are thrown into the main area, the players throw over the heads of their opponents to those of their number behind the line.

(4) The two try to hit their opponents below the knee.

(5) If hit below the knee, players join their team members behind the line, and try to get opponents out.

(6) Balls may be interrupted as they are thrown over opposing team.

(7) If any player crosses a line unlawfully to get the ball, a free pass is given to the opposing side.

(8) The game may continue until everyone is out, on one side or the other.

8 END BALL

You will require two or more balls.

All details are exactly the same as for the above game with one major difference: the aim is to score goals. A 'goal' is scored when a ball is 'clearly' caught by a player in the tramlines. The player catching the ball must have both feet in the tramlines, and must not overbalance. Players in the tramlines are changed at intervals.

Both games are usually more successful when girls and boys are separated, as the boys tend to do most of the work when teams are mixed.

9 FIVE (OR TEN) PASSES

You will need a large ball.

The players stand in a wide circle, with one player in the centre to intercept ball if possible. Pass large ball around or across circle, counting passes. The object is to make five (or ten) passes without the ball being intercepted.

Any age, but especially 11+.

10 FOOTBALL ROUNDERS

You will need equipment as for Rounders.

Play this game exactly as Rounders, except that you have a wicket about a yard wide, and you have to kick the ball. Danish Rounders can be played in this way also.

11 HAYLO

You will need two chairs, two sticks and a Haylo ring.

Teams should be of the same age approximately and not more than fifteen to twenty in a team. The length of pitch should vary from thirty yards, depending on age. At each end is a chair on which stands a member of the team playing towards that goal. He has a stick in his hand. Round the chair is marked off a circular area, diameter three yards. The aim is to throw a Haylo ring over the stick. The one who catches it must not lose his balance in so doing and fall off the chair. A pass must be made when a player is touched; and no player can shoot after being touched. There are no side lines or back line; but running a long way away must be discouraged. Never allow rough play. To start the game and in any dispute throw up the quoit between two players, who on catching it, pass it to one of their own side.

12 INFORMAL SKITTLE BALL

You will need ball and skittles.

This is a simple quick-moving game with few rules, suitable for either indoor or outdoor play. The court is marked as shown in the diagram opposite. The object of the game is to throw the ball and to knock down the opponents' skittle. The rules are simple:

(1)   The ball must be passed by hand. It may not be carried for more than two paces nor held for more than two seconds. It may be dribbled, however, by pat-bouncing, or by volleying with the hands.

(2)   No tackling or rough play of any kind is permitted.

(3)   The goalkeeper must remain inside the

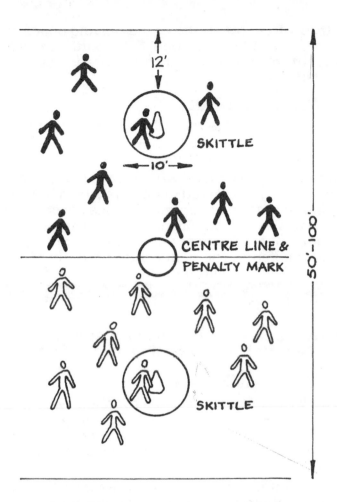

INFORMAL SKITTLE BALL
(SKITTLES ABOUT 2' HIGH)

circle. Attackers must on no account step into the circle.

(4) A skittle knocked down by the attackers scores two points. If knocked down by the defending goalkeeper one point is scored by the opposition.

(5) For any infringement of rules 2 and 3 a pen-

alty throw from the centre of the playing space at an unguarded skittle is awarded. If the skittle is knocked down from a penalty throw, three points are awarded.

13 NATURE TRAIL

You will need a tape measure for each team.
Played in a garden preferably with trees. Two or more teams of equal number each.

Having elected a captain who always stays at home base, teams go in search of objects which they have to bring back to their captain. The leader calls three objects at a time, e.g. a 50 mm blade of grass, an elm leaf, a feather. Players are given one minute or less to find the items. The next group of items are then called. Points are allotted for each correct item. A referee ensures fair play and accurate measurements! The game is played in silence. It can be further complicated by adding 'burdens' to the collectors, e.g. carrying a team member on the search piggy-back fashion or hopping on one foot, etc.

14 NET HAND BALL

You will require one frido or football, two sets of posts. These are made out of two upright posts 8 feet above ground with a distance between of 6 feet. Two cross bars are fixed to the posts at a space of approx. 3 feet.

The net is attached to the post by means of hooks on cross members and upright. The net should be of adequate proportions to allow a pouch to be formed to hold a ball when thrown into it.
Pitch: 150 ft. × 100 ft., larger or smaller according to age group. Goal areas 15 ft. × 20 ft. are marked and a centre circle of 2 feet.
Teams. Any number of players equally divided into two teams. One goalkeeper is elected for each team. They alone are allowed inside the goal areas. The teams take up positions in their own half of the field, two centre-forwards stand outside centre circle fac-

22

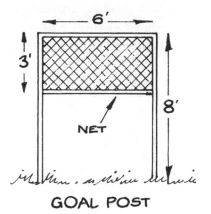

GOAL POST

ing opponents' goal. The referee throws the ball above them and they can jump to gain possession; the ball is in play when one of them has touched it. Players endeavour to advance towards opponents' goal by running with the ball or by passing. Immediately a player in possession is touched he must pass the ball. He cannot score if he is touched immediately before shooting.

Rules. Kicking, pushing and fisting are not allowed. Rough play must also be penalized. A free

DIAGRAM OF PITCH (NOT TO SCALE)

pass at the place of the offence is given for these and other infringements of similar nature – for free passes or penalties all players must stand at least three yards away from thrower.

When a ball crosses the side lines a player from the opposite side shall throw in. A ball crossing the goal-line, after being touched by an attacker, shall be thrown in by the goalkeeper from the point where the goal circle joins the goal-line. When the ball is touched by a defender a corner throw shall be taken by an attacker standing at the extreme corner of the pitch on the side at which the ball went out.

15 RAGGER

You will need a tennis ball.

Divide the children into two teams. The pitch can be any length over 50 yards. Mark out two goals 4 or 5 yards wide. Mark out a semicircle around them 15 yards in radius. A player may run with the ball until touched, when he must pass at once and underhand only. Goals are scored from *outside* the area by throwing the ball past the goalkeeper, who is the only man on either side allowed in the area. Once a player is touched he cannot shoot. To start the game, and in any dispute, the ball is bounced between the two rival players. After it is bounced they tap it backwards to a member on their own side. The referee should not allow any rough play.

Variation: **Touch Rugby.**
This is a similar game, but scoring is by touching the ball down behind the goal-line with one or both hands (a try). Use a Rugby ball.

16 ROUNDERS

You will need rounders sticks, rounders ball or tennis ball. Four bases or posts.
Two teams of nine players are needed.

Procedure
One team bats whilst the opponents field. Fielders

are given positions: bowler, backstop, 1st, 2nd, 3rd and 4th bases, 1st, 2nd and 3rd deeps. Bowler bowls underarm to the batsman – the ball must be between shoulder and knee level. The batsman must run to first base whether or not he hits the ball. He is out if the ball is caught or the base to which he is running is stumped before he reaches it. If the batsman hits the ball and runs round the pitch he gains a rounder. If he gets around without having first hit the ball he scores half a rounder.

The team continues batting until everyone is out. At no time must there be more than one batsman at a base. If this occurs, the first batsman to have arrived at the base is out. Batsman must stop running from base to base as soon as the bowler has the ball and is standing in the bowler's square.

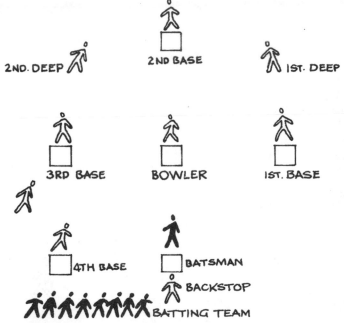

Fielders must have the ball in their possession and must be in contact with the base in order to get a batsman out. Two innings are usually played in rounders.

25

17   SHINTY

You will need a shinty stick for each player and a hockey ball.

This is a game suitable for twenty to forty players. It is similar to hockey but there are fewer rules. A pitch is marked out and goal areas indicated. Players are divided into two equal teams. Centres and goal-keepers are appointed. At the start of play teams are arranged in their own half. The two centres bully off, and teams attempt to score goals by passing the ball to each other and into the goal. Rules can be intro-duced as necessary, e.g. sticks must not be raised above shoulder level.

18   SWEDISH LONG BALL

You will need a small ball.

An area of approx. 100 ft. × 50 ft. should be marked off.

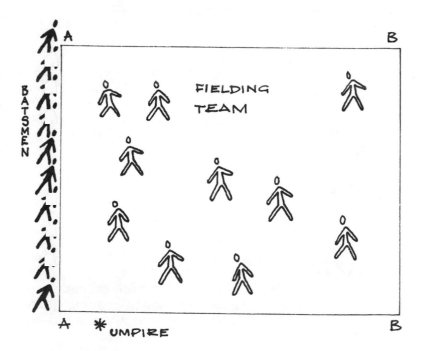

The aim is to score as many runs as possible. A run is scored by getting from A to B and back to A.

The teams stand as indicated in the diagram. The game proceeds as follows:

(1)   The umpire throws the ball up at point X.

(2)   The first player hits the ball with his hand before it bounces.

(3)   As soon as the ball is hit he begins running towards B. If he reaches B safely but does not think he can get back, or if the ball is in the umpire's hands, he may stay there (if the latter, he *must* stay there), and then can run back after someone else has hit the ball – this will *not* count as a run.

(4)   The characteristic of this game is that if one person is out, then the whole team is out. For this reason the game is very fast-moving.

(5)   A player is out if he hits the ball behind the line, if he hits a catch and is caught, or if a player in the opposing team picks up the ball (he may not move with it, only pass or throw it) and hits anyone on the other side running between A and B. Once behind the line players are safe, but they must run when they have hit the ball.

(6)   If the side is out in any of the above ways, the umpire then shouts 'All change'. The fielding team then runs to *either* end to safety behind the lines A and B. The ball must be *put* down by the fielding side for the following reason: if the outgoing batting side are quick enough to pick up the ball and hit another opponent with it before that opponent gets behind the line, then the umpire again calls 'All change'.

(7)   Those who run behind the non-batting line after changing may go to batting end any time, providing the ball is in play, i.e. when it has been hit by another batsman. Once at the batting end players remain lined up there until it is their turn to bat. Even if a player scores a run, he does not have another bat, the next person has a turn.

(8)   When the ball is in the umpire's hands it is dead.

(9)   It is advisable to have two or three people to

27

aid and abet the umpire. It is also advisable to introduce the rules gradually, and not all at one fell swoop.

19 THREE-COURT DODGE BALL

You will need a small ball.

The playing space is marked out as shown below, the centre space being somewhat larger than the two end spaces to allow the dodgers more freedom of movement. The players are then divided into three equal groups, two of the groups being throwers, the third being the dodgers. The two end teams try to hit the dodgers in the centre space below knee height with a small ball. A count is kept of all successful hits. Each team occupies the centre space for the same length of time, say, three minutes, and the team which has been hit the least number of times is the winner.

ATTACKERS   DODGERS   ATTACKERS

20'-35'

20 THROW IT AND RUN

You will need four balls, a hoop or rope, two skittles

for each group, four bean bags or balls in a circle (hoop or rope circle).

The thrower throws all four balls out as far as he can and then begins to run between two skittles. The fielders pass the four balls back to the circle; when all four are back, shout 'Stop!' See how many 'runs' the thrower has scored.

Variation. The thrower may see how many fielders he can touch before all four balls are back in the circle.

21 VOLLEY BALL

You will need a volley ball, and a badminton net or a rope stretched across the centre of the court at a height of 8 feet. You will also need a volley ball court marked out – size approximately 50 ft. × 30 ft.

Rules

(1)   Divide sixteen players into two teams and give them positions as in the diagram.

1	8	7	6
2	3	4	5
5	4	3	2
6	7	8	1

(2)   Toss for service or choice of side.

(3)   No. 1 player serves the ball from behind the back line by batting the ball with his fist in an underarm movement.

(4)   If the service hits the net or fails to reach the opponents' side, the team is out and service goes to the opponents.

(5)   If the ball touches the ground on the opponents' side the serving team scores a point.

(6) Players keep the ball up by batting it with their hands. Any number of players may bat the ball before it is returned over the net, but no player may bat the ball more than once in succession, neither may a player catch or hold the ball.

(7) Only the serving side can score.

(8) When a service is lost the team moves into a new position (see diagram), No. 1 moving into No. 8, No. 2 into No. 1 position, and the opponents begin service.

(9) The first team to reach fifteen points wins the game.

Variation. A simpler form of this game is to have two groups of children (not necessarily sixteen) on each side of the net and give them a service order, but don't give them special positions, only encourage some to play forward and some to play back.

SECTION 2
GAMES WITHOUT
EQUIPMENT

1 ARMADAS

Partners with knees bent sit on each other's feet, as shown in the diagram, and hold each other's shoulders. (For method of movement see *Galleons*, p. 32). Two teams of eight or more 'galleons' are formed. The galleons line up along each end of the playing space, and at a given signal move toward each other and try to upset the opposing galleons. A galleon is 'wrecked' if it rolls over on to its side, or if either of the two players forming it places a hand on the ground. The game can be played until all the ships of one side are eliminated, or for a given time, the side with the most pairs unwrecked being the winner.

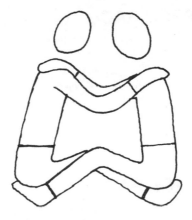

Variations on Armadas: All the ships line up at one end of the room and race to the opposite end. Or: the ships are evenly spaced round a very large circle. Each one then tries to catch and bump the one in front. If successful, in the next race the ship moves up one place.

2 BOAT RACE

A 'boat' consists of eight or ten players in knees-full-bend position, each holding the shoulder of the player in front. Facing the players is a 'cox' who stands and holds the hands of the front player. The boat moves forward by all the players springing together off both feet, the cox assisting by calling out the rhythm. The activity should be made competitive, one boat racing against two or three more. During a race, any boat which founders, i.e. breaks into two or more parts, is eliminated.

3 CATERPILLAR WALK

Players take position as shown. Hands must be kept still and legs stiff.

1   2   3

4 CENTIPEDE RACE

This is done in pairs, as shown.

5 DUCK FIGHTING

Players crouch in pairs, as shown. Keeping still themselves, they try to make the opponent lose balance by pushing his hands. This is a static balance activity. It can be made dynamic by allowing the pairs to hop or spring about while trying to unbalance each other.

6 GALLEONS

This is an extremely amusing activity which can be developed into the game of *Armadas.* Partners with knees bent sit on each other's feet as shown in the diagram for *Armadas*, and hold each other's shoulders. They start a rocking movement. As one rises slightly from the ground the other slides the feet forward a short distance, then as the other in turn lifts, the first draws his feet backwards a little, a forward movement being obtained. With practice this movement can be made relatively quickly and in almost any direction. When the movement has been learned, the activity can be made competitive, and pairs can race against others over short distances.

7 SOLDIERS AND BRIGANDS

Players stand in two lines – one soldiers, with backs turned; the other brigands, who creep forward on tiptoe towards the soldiers. When a yard or two away from the soldiers, the brigands 'open fire' (clap hands and stamp feet). The soldiers then turn and chase the brigands. Those caught before passing over the base line become soldiers and join in the chasing at the next game.

8 STRONGMAN

Two teams.

Numbered teams stand facing each other, as far as possible matched for size and weight. When a number is called the two contestants seek to lift each other off the ground. No holds barred but careful umpiring is necessary to insure no violence occurs! Both feet must be clear of the ground for the lifter to be awarded a point.

9 WIZARD CHAIN GANG

Players scattered around large lawn or field. A Press-gang man is chosen who whizzes around the playing area catching victims. Once touched they join the press-gang by linking arms. Escaping players are gradually caught and join on. The last person untouched is the winner.

SECTION 3
CHASING AND RUNNING GAMES

1 CIRCLE NUMBER CHASE

All the players stand in a circle and number off by fours, fives, or sixes, according to the number taking part. The leader then calls out a number, say, 'five'. Immediately all the 'fives' chase each other in clockwise direction round the outside of the circle and try to tag the one in front, and at the same time avoid being tagged by the person behind. Each number should be called an equal number of times, and the player with the greatest number of tags to his credit is the winner.

2 COLLECTION RELAY

The course is marked out as shown in the diagram below. The leader runs from the start line over the line AB. He then runs back and grasps the hand of No. 2. They both run over the line AB, and then both go back to pick up the third man. Three now run together over the course, and three go back to pick up the fourth man, and so on until all six are over the line AB. The same process is repeated in the opposite direction, but this time No. 6 is the one to start the return journey. The race is complete when all the team is back to its original starting position.

3 COPS AND ROBBERS

Any even number of players. A Cop and a Robber are selected. The rest form lines and hold hands. Streets and Alleyways, down which the cop must chase the robber, are made by the lines of children. The chase ensues with the leader occasionally calling out 'change'. All the 'street players' make a quarter turn and immediately link up again. The streets now run in opposite directions. The cop and robber have to adjust themselves to the new pattern each time. The unbreakable rule is that neither of the two is ever allowed to pass through the players with linked hands.

4 CROSS-OVER RELAY

You will need one small ball, or bean bag, per team.

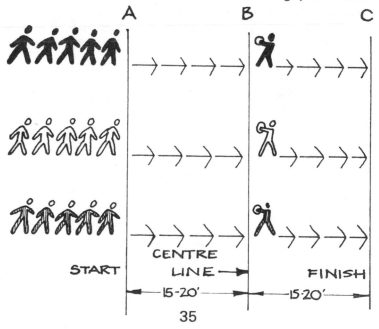

35

Three chalk lines are drawn at distances apart suitable to the age of the players and the accommodation available. A convenient size is shown for older performers (see diagram). The leader, holding the ball, runs forward to the centre line, turns round, throws the ball to the next in the line, and then takes up a position behind line C. The race normally finishes when the last player is over the finishing line, though, if desired, the return journey can be made in a similar manner, with the team finishing behind the starting line.

5 HADRIAN'S WALL

A court is marked out as shown in the diagram below. The wall should be about 3 or 4 yards across. The defenders stand in this area, while the attackers stand in one of the neutral spaces. When the captain of the defenders calls 'Go', the attackers try to cross the wall and reach safety on the opposite side. The defenders try to tag the attackers within the wall area, and they are not permitted to leave the wall. Anyone tagged while on the wall automatically becomes defender. The last untagged player wins the game and becomes the captain of the new defenders of the wall.

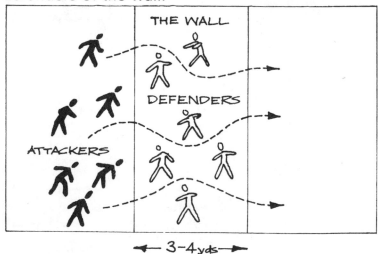

6 KEEP THE BASKET FULL

You will need fifteen to twenty tennis or small rubber balls, a box or basket.

The leader has a box or basket in which the balls are placed. As quickly as possible he picks one ball at a time out of the box and rolls them across the playing space. The players race after the balls, retrieve them and place them back in the box, the aim being never to let the box, or basket, become empty. The game should be played for two or three minutes only, or until the box is emptied, whichever is the less time.

7 INDIAN FILE DODGE BALL

You will need one ball.

The players arrange themselves as shown in the diagram. Inside the circle of players five or six arrange themselves in file, grasping each other round the waist or on the shoulders. The whole file is free to move in any direction, but the grip must not be broken. The circle of players endeavours to hit

INDIAN FILE DODGE BALL

with a ball the back player of the file below knee height. The ball should be passed around or across the circle to a player best situated to throw, and not just thrown haphazardly by anyone. The person scoring a hit goes to the front of the file and the one hit takes his place in the circle.

8   KINGS AND SOLDIERS

You will need four bundles of coloured bands.

Four kings, each with bundles of coloured bands, chase the rest of the players, to capture their 'army'. When the king catches someone, he gives him a band to wear. He joins in chasing, and brings his captors to the king for their bands. The king rounds up his army when all bands have been given out, and races to finishing line (or corner).

9   RUNNING VERSUS THROWING RELAY

You will need one small ball, or bean bag, per team.

This is a combination of an ordinary running relay and a throwing relay. Teams are arranged as shown in diagram. One team stands equally spaced round a large chalked circle, while the team leader stands in the centre holding the bean bag or ball. The other team stands in single file with its leader on a chalked starting line. On the starting signal the leader of the A team passes the ball to each member of his team in turn. As he receives the return throw from each one he calls out the number of good passes made. The B team in the meantime are racing, relay fashion, round the circle. The moment the last runner is back, the number of passes made by the throwing team is noted, say, fifty-three. The teams then change over, and the new throwing team endeavours to make more than fifty-three passes before the new running team completes its course. The running team, of course, endeavours to finish before the throwing team reaches fifty-three passes.

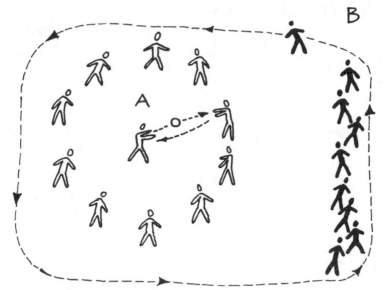

10 SPACE SHIPS

A game suitable for 7-11 year olds. Mark out an area as in the diagram below. The nose-cone is out of bounds, and anyone who touches it is eliminated, as is anyone who touches the space outside the spacecraft. The leader shouts out a section of the space ship. The children must get there as fast as possible, the last one, two or three being eliminated. Other special orders can include 'Emergency', when the children sit down with head between knees; 'Prepare for take-off', when they lie down on their faces facing the nose-cone; and 'Prepare for landing', when they lie down facing the stern. Probably thirty to fifty is the maximum number for this game, but this depends on the size of the area.

	COCKPIT	MOTOR	
NOSE			STERN
	RADIO	ROCKETS	

11 WHEEL RELAY

You will need one ball, baton, or bean bag, per team.

Teams arrange themselves as shown in the diagram. The player numbered 'six' in each team, holds the object. On the starting signal the object is passed down the team to No. 1 who then races round the wheel, as shown, finishing in the place originally occupied by No. 6 (who now becomes No. 5). The object is passed down the line again, and No. 2 now runs. This continues until the original No. 6 returns to the place he first occupied. The object is then passed down to No. 1, who, the moment he receives it, holds it aloft to indicate that his team has finished.

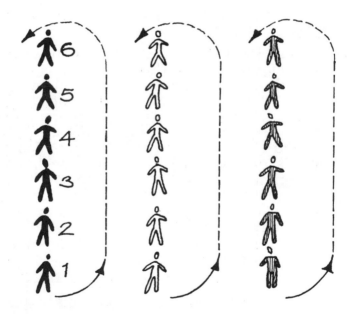

12 SIAMESE TWIN TAG

All the players form pairs. One of the pair stands as close as possible behind the other and grasps him round the waist. This close position must be maintained during all movement, which, of course, necessitates both members of the pairs always keeping in step with each other. One pair is selected as chaser, and the game continues in normal fashion. Groups of three, four, and five can be made if necessary.

13 SWINGING ROPE

You will need a piece of string or rope, about 10 feet long, weighted at one end.

All players stand in a circle except one, an adult, who stands in the centre holding the weighted rope. He starts to swing it round, gradually raising the height. Players are eliminated as they fail to jump over the rope.

14 TEAM TAG

The players are divided into teams all of equal number. One team is selected to act as chasers. A given time, say, two minutes, is allowed for the chasing team to tag as many of the other players as possible. When a person is tagged, he or she must stand still. At the end of the period allowed the tags are counted. Each team in turn acts as chaser. The team with the greatest number of tags is the winner.

15 STATIONS (improved tag game)

A competition played in groups. You need a minimum of 5 groups or maximum 9 groups, with an equal number of competitors. Best age group 7–12 years.

They sit in allotted places – circles of chairs or circles marked on sand or grass.

One group is selected as 'catchers'. Each group is given the name of a station. The organiser calls the names of two stations and these groups change places, hopefully without getting tagged by the catchers. Any competitor who is touched joins the organiser. The winner is the group with the most players left in when time is up. That group then becomes the 'catchers'.

Variation.
Groups can be named after planets, stars or pop stars. The name of the game can be changed accordingly.

SECTION 4
WIDE AND HUNT
GAMES

There are many variations of a basically similar game. The idea is to get the children, either individually or in teams, moving round from one helper (camp officer) to another until they find some treasure, or return to the helper from whom they started. The helpers are spread out over quite a large area, and each gives a clue, usually, as to the whereabouts of the next helper. Here are some variations:

1 BLAST OFF

This is a good seaside or field game. Played in groups of mixed ages. Work to a prepared script to be adapted to local conditions and age of participants. When one group has completed an exercise, award points and move on to the next instruction. A leader from each group carries the instructions and a referee is in charge of each team to insure completion of each order. The sample scripts below are self-explanatory.

Blast Off Sample Script 1

1. In order to take off each team member must find a piece of wood.
2. You are now in space, your crew has become weightless. Collect 6 stones each at least as big as your fist.
3. It is time for your first meal; collect some seaweed for each member of your crew.
4. Your space ship is being invaded. Make a hole big enough for all your crew to hide in.
5. Your captain has gone down with a fever and needs water. Fetch your captain some water in a container of some kind. He needs at least a cup full.
6. All your crew over 9 years have caught a mysterious disease. The rest of the crew or the captain must carry them over 18 metres.
7. You are nearing Mars and need to decelerate; all hop backwards.
8. Your spaceship has landed on Mars. The ground is very hot. The captain must wheelbarrow half the team to the banner. The rest collect 3 shells.
9. Find your landing area and dig for 10 precious stones (e.g. precious stones can be wrapped sweets or prizes. The number depending on size of team).

Blast Off Sample Script 2

(A life on the ocean wave)

1. Having made up your crew, collect a stick or twig and make a flag.
2. Before setting sail you need to collect enough stores:
   1 insect for meat
   10 flowers for dessert
   Plenty of seaweed for vegetables (biggest pile bonus points)
3. Half the crew are down with scurvy. Collect as many kinds of green leaf as you can.
4. Pirates are sighted on the forward beam. Collect stones over 6 inches for cannon balls. Each sailor needs 3 cannon balls.

43

5. The ship is sinking. Every sailor needs some driftwood to cling to.

6. Create an island big enough for all your crew to stand on.

7. The sun is getting very hot. Build a hut to protect the smallest member of your crew.

8. While exploring the island you see the pirates' ship, but their camp is surrounded by a big wall. You have to climb over the wall without being seen by the guards. Those caught will be shot on sight. All wounded sailors must be carried in future.

9. Over the wall you see a fire in the distance and guards round a long trench. Advance cautiously and use your eyes for further directions.

2 CROOKS

Each worker is a crook with a funny name. They are spread out over a wide area, and each team of children is given a different name to ask for first. When they find the helper who responds to this name, he gives them another name, until they have completed the full circle and returned to the starting-point.

3 HAT GAME

Half the helpers put on funny hats and spread out round the area. Each has one question and one answer. Teams of children, with up to six in each team, and led by an unhatted helper, if desired, are told to find one of the hatted helpers (each team to a different hatted helper) from whom to get their first question. Questions are for information that can be obtained in the area in which the hatted helper stands. They are of the sort, 'Who lives at No. 84 Marsh Lane?' Having found the answer, the team goes round to all the hatted helpers until it finds the one who responds to that answer with a further question. On returning to the first hatted helper, the team is sent back to the starting-point, and the first team there is the winner.

4 HUNT THE HELPER

This is suitable for all ages except the under-sevens, unless escorted in groups by helpers. After the children have assembled at a central point, the helpers go in disguise to their various places in the area. They must have pencils. The children are divided into pairs, each with a piece of paper. They are told to challenge the helpers with some stupid and embarrassing password which is aimed at deterring them from saying it to everyone they see. They are given a fixed time, 30 to 45 minutes, depending on the size and suitability of the area, in which to collect as many initials from the helpers as possible. They should be told to do this as quietly as possible so as not to attract other children to the same helper. The helpers can be hard to find, but not totally hidden, as this is not purely 'hide and seek'. At the end of the given time all helpers should proceed to the central spot, as should all the children, and the pair with the most signatures is the winner.

5 INFORMATION COLLECTING

Groups of children can be given lists of information, preferably useful, to collect in a local area. The first groups to return with all the information required are the winners.

6 NIGEL'S NAVY

You will need four small balls of different coloured wool, and some white cards.

This is suitable for all ages and any number. Divide the children into three or four fleets. Each has a helper as Admiral and Quartermaster. Each also has a base in which the quartermaster sits. There are three types of ships: battleships, submarines and destroyers. There should be three destroyers to every two submarines and to every one battleship. Each child should be given a small piece of white card with the letter D, S, or B, to show which ship they represent. Each fleet has its own colour, and

45

each child in the fleet has a piece of wool of that colour tied to his wrist. During the battle a battleship takes a destroyer; a destroyer takes a submarine; and a submarine takes a battleship. These facts should be made very clear to the children. At a given signal the fleets are released from base to central fighting area, where every member challenges any other member of another fleet by touching them. Each then says what ship he represents. Nothing happens if they are the same, but when different, the loser must give up his piece of wool to the other, and return to base for a new piece of wool from the quartermaster. He *may not continue fighting* without a piece of wool of his own colour. The side collecting the most wool of other colours wins. It is advisable to have half-time in order to change the children into different ships by giving them different cards.

One of the battleships is given an extra card, which signifies the flag that it carries, for he is the flag ship. This flag must be made the decisive factor, and so, depending on the number of children in each fleet, worth at least 50 to 150 pieces of wool. If this battleship is attacked by a submarine it must surrender its flag as well, which the submarine at once returns to his admiral, who at once gives it to his own flag ship, who thus becomes doubly valuable. This flag ship, if attacked, loses both its flags at the same time. Clearly it is wise for the flag ship to play a defensive role and to be helped out by defending submarines and destroyers of its own fleet. The flag ship child can only be changed at half-time. The game can be played for up to thirty minutes by virtually any numbers. The arduous job of counting the wool should be left to the end, when all the children hand in their captured wool to their quartermasters.

7 PRISONER'S BASE

A chalk or a string line should be drawn across the middle of the playing area. On each side of this line a camp is formed, and also a place for prisoners.

Give names to the sides, say Ducks and Drakes. The game is started by one side, say the Ducks, crossing the boundary line and challenging the Drakes to catch them. The Drakes set off in pursuit, but if a Drake crosses the boundary line on to the Duck side, he can then be caught by a Duck. When a player is caught he is carried off to the prisoners' base of the opposing team. He can be rescued by one of his team mates venturing into enemy territory to release him by touching him. Obviously this is dangerous because the prisoners will be well guarded.

The game is won by the side which captures all the members of the opposing team. In fact this rarely happens if the teams are well matched, because there is a continual exchange of prisoners, and excitement remains high throughout the game. It may be best to set a time-limit for finishing the game.

8 ROCKETS AND INTERCEPTORS

You will need some coloured bands, six tins, and a number of bottle-tops or dried peas.

This game is suitable for all ages, but the main problem is the area, which needs to be partly open and partly of the kind where children can hide themselves, i.e. with bushes and little hillocks. The children are divided into two teams, Rockets and Interceptors, each with their own coloured bands. They are Rockets for the first half of the game, and then the same team are Interceptors for the second half of the game.

About six target areas are laid out in the playing area as wide apart as possible. They should be about 10 yards in diameter each, and have a helper as umpire at or near each end, and a tin or receptacle in the middle. Only the Rockets are allowed in this area, and no more than four Interceptors are allowed to hover around the area. Each Rocket is given five war-heads, i.e. bottle-tops, dried peas, or some suitable small object. If so desired, special war-heads can be issued worth five bottle-tops each. Five of these should be given to one or two chosen Rockets, and those who have them should have no ordinary war-heads worth one each.

The aim of the Rockets is to destroy the target areas by landing a fixed number of war-heads in them, say, twenty-five for each target area. A bonus of ten points (=war-heads) or more can be given for each target area wholly destroyed. The Rockets have to run into the target areas without being touched by an Interceptor. If they are so touched they must give up one of their war-heads (worth five each). Several helpers should be spread around as umpires. A fixed time for the game should be arranged. One team is Rockets for the first twenty minutes, say, and the other team for the next twenty minutes. Whichever team lands the most war-heads, plus bonus points, in that time is the winner.

9 SCAVENGER HUNT

The children are divided into pairs or teams, and they are given a list of objects to collect in a specified time. The first children to return with all the objects are the winners. The objects would depend on local surroundings – particular flowers, leaves, grasses, insects, shells, pebbles, etc., can be collected.

10 TREASURE HUNT

A simple form of treasure hunt is merely to send groups of children from one helper to another by giving them clues, until the last helper sends them to the treasure. A variation on this is to tell them they are catching a spy, and the clues lead them to run him to ground at a certain place. Children must challenge the spy with an amusing password before he reveals his identity. He is, of course, one of the helpers in hiding.

11 WATER WIDE GAME

You will need plenty of marbles or peas, say 100.
Squeezy bottles for most players, plenty of water,
two colours of breakable wool.
Any number of participants up to 60.

Procedure.
Two teams defend a base, about 4 yards radius, no
one being allowed in his own base except to get a
new life. Wool is tied around the wrist of all players–
this constitutes a life. The two teams are disting-
uished by coloured wool. The bases are about 200
yards apart and not hidden. If you reach your
opponents' base, wool intact, you can take a marble.
If your wool 'life' is taken on the way back you must
surrender your marble. The team with most marbles
at the end is the winner. The duration of the game is
dependent on local conditions.

Water squirting.
Water squirting is a means of defence. Make sure
plenty of water is available. Squirting water in the
opponents' eyes may slow them down, but apart
from this the water squirting is in fact irrelevant.
Hence, teenagers can pick on their leaders and soak
them utterly! If there aren't enough squeezy bottles
to go round, one can make it a rule that capturing
enemy bottles is allowed.

SECTION 5
SUGGESTIONS
FOR SPORTS DAY

1 CAMEL RACE

Groups of three children. One is the head, another
makes the back and holds the waist of the 'head', the
third is the rider, who is seated. This can be played

49

with the 'head' blindfolded being steered by the rider, but this variation is for older children only.

2 COLLECTION RACE

You will need some artificial flowers.

Scatter over the course artificial flowers of various colours. The children collect four of any specified colour on the way to the winning post. This race can be run using coloured wool or string.

3 DWARF RACE

Line up as many children as required and give them a short course to race over. Each child grasps his ankles, and must keep the hold until the winning line is crossed.

4 EGG AND SPOON RACE

You will need a spoon and a potato or ball for each competitor.

The spoon and the potato or ball are placed on the ground in front of the competitor. On the signal he picks up the spoon, and with it picks up the 'egg' (potato or ball), and runs to the finishing line. He must not touch the 'egg' by hand.

5 HOT BRICKS

You will need a number of bricks or flower-pots.

Competitors walk a measured course on bricks or inverted flower-pots, without putting their feet to the ground.

6 OBSTACLE RACE

You will need a variety of obstacles.

This race is usually played off in teams grouped by age. Any variety of obstacles can be arranged over a given course, making sure that they are compatible with the ability of any given group. Suggestions are as follows:

(1)   Crawling under a tarpaulin which is pegged to the ground.
(2)   Crawling through large pipes.
(3)   Passing through suspended car tyres.
(4)   Walking a plank.
(5)   Eating a cream cracker and drinking a glass of water.
(6)   Finding a Smartie sweet in a saucer of flour (no hands allowed, use mouth only).

7   POTATO RACE

You will need a number of buckets or other containers, and some potatoes or large stones.

Each competitor stands on the starting line near to a bucket (or container). In front of him is a line of potatoes (or stones) spaced at yard intervals. On the signal competitors run and pick up a potato and return it to their buckets. This is repeated, and the first person to put all his potatoes in his bucket is the winner.

8   POTTER SPORTS OR MINI SPORTS

You will need a number of articles such as are given in 'Suggestions' below.

This is suitable for all ages. Divide the children into small teams, and have several events of the funfair variety laid out, the same number as you have teams. Start each team with a different event, and give five minutes at it in which to amass as many points as possible. Blow a whistle after five minutes to make the team move on to the next event. Allow a two minute gap between events to explain the rules of each. One helper is needed on each event, and he keeps the score for each team. Suggestions are as follows:
(1)   Throw ping-pong balls into numbered egg cartons.
(2)   Pick up grains of rice with hair-pin.
(3)   Throw bal!s into numbered buckets or other containers.

(4) Drop 1p coins into bucket of water to cover 5p or ½p coin.
(5) Aim a ball at a row of cans.
(6) Build a tower of matchsticks.
(7) Pick up peas with a drinking straw.

9 SACK RACE

You will need a sack for each competitor.

On the signal the competitor gets into the sack and jumps to the finishing line.

10 SEDAN CHAIR RACE

Competitors are in groups of three, two making a seat by joining hands, on which the third sits and is carried along. The distance of the course will depend on the age-group of the participants.

11 SLOW BICYCLE RACE

Each competitor rides his bicycle over a specified course. The last at the finishing line is the winner. If a competitor puts a foot to the ground he is penalized by losing a point or advancing two yards.

12 RUGBY SCRUM

You will need a tape for a dividing line.

Two even teams 'set down' into a scrum rugby fashion over a dividing line. The team pushing their opponents over the line are the winners. This must be played at least twice so that the teams can change ends.

13 THREE-LEGGED RACE

You will need a handkerchief or scarf for each two competitors.

The children are paired, and their inside legs tied together just above the ankle. On the signal all the pairs run to the finishing line.

14 TUG OF WAR

You will need a strong rope.

This is always popular and a 'crowd enthuser'. Helpers and teachers against Mums and Dads, or adults against children, can be matched.

15 WHEELBARROW RACE

The children are paired. One child walks on hands while his partner holds his legs up. The course should be fairly short.

16 WELLY THROWING

You will need a wellington boot

Same as discus throwing.
A wellington boot substitutes for discus. The player with the longest throw is the winner. Handicaps e.g. throwing with left hand or one hand in trouser pocket, can be introduced for variation.

17 WHEELRIGHT

You will need lengths of string or tape approximately 15 metres, a bicycle and a referee for each team.

Divide players into teams of about 10 persons. Stretch the lines out, making a track, leaving at least 1 metre between each. Teams line up with one bicycle. On the command 'go' No 1 team leader picks up the bicycle and wheels it down the line. It must always have its wheels on the line; any default and the judge sends the player back to start again.

   Having completed the course, the player rides the cycle back to his team and the rest of the players follow the pattern one by one, until the whole team has completed the race.

Variations.
1.   Use small, strong cycles for adults – the riding return can be humorous.
2.   Run the race as a relay dividing each team into halves. This speeds up the process.

53

3. Work in pairs. A lady sitting on the cycle, without using pedals, the man providing the power for movement and balance. Even more fun if the man is blindfolded! Only recommended for younger couples.

SECTION 6A
INDOOR GAMES
FOR VERY YOUNG
CHILDREN

1 BALL CATCHING
You will need a large ball.

Children stand in a circle (about eight to ten). Leader stands in the middle with a large ball which he throws to children in turn. When a child drops the ball, he has a turn in the middle.

2 CATCHING TAILS
You will need pieces of braid, one for each pair.

The children are paired. One child has a 'tail' (piece of braid) tucked at the back. At a signal the children with 'tails' rush off. The others follow them and try to catch a 'tail'. When a 'tail' is caught, they skip around together holding the braid.

3 FARMER'S IN HIS DEN
The children form a circle, with one in the middle as 'farmer'. They sing:

> The farmer's in his den,
> The farmer's in his den,
> E.I.E.I.O.,
> The farmer's in his den.

Then:

> The farmer wants a wife,
> The farmer wants a wife etc.

and the child in the centre picks a 'wife' from the children in the circle (sex immaterial!).

Then:

> The wife wants a child, etc.

and the 'wife' in the centre picks a 'child' from the children in the circle.

Then:

> The child wants a nurse, etc.

and the 'child' in the centre picks a 'nurse' from the children in the circle.

Then:

> The nurse wants a dog, etc.

and the 'nurse' in the centre picks a 'dog' from the children in the circle.

Then:

> The dog wants a bone, etc.,

the last verse being

> We all pat the dog, etc.,

and the children in the circle move towards the centre and endeavour to pat the 'dog'.

4 FLOPPY BUNNIES

All the children pretend to be bunnies, hopping about the room with their hands at the side of their heads to make big ears. When the leader calls out 'Here comes the hunter!' they must all immediately stop moving and keep absolutely still until the leader calls out 'The hunter's gone!' when they can start hopping again. They should be kept still for about five to ten seconds. Any child wobbling or falling over in that time is out of the game, which continues until only one player – the winner – is left in.

5 HERE WE COME LUBIN LOO

The children in a circle dance round singing:

> Here we come Lubin Loo,
> Here we come Lubin Lay,

Here we come Lubin Loo,
All on a Saturday night.
Variations: Put your right hand in,
Put your right hand out,
Put your right hand in,
All on a Saturday night.
(the children doing the actions as they sing the words).
Put your left hand in, etc.
Put your left leg in, etc.
Put your head in, etc.
Put your whole body in, etc.
(with the appropriate actions).

6 HERE WE GO ROUND THE MULBERRY BUSH
(or Christmas Tree, as in season)

The children dance round in a circle singing:
Here we go round the mulberry bush,
The mulberry bush, the mulberry bush.
Here we go round the mulberry bush
On a cold and frosty morning.
Variations:
This is the way we clap our hands, etc.
This is the way we stamp our feet, etc.
This is the way we shake our heads, etc.
(with actions).

7 HUNTING WE WILL GO

The children in two lines facing each other sing:
A-hunting we will go,
A-hunting we will go,
We'll catch a fox and
Put him in a box,
And never let him go.
They clap as they sing. Then the first two partners skip down the line, holding hands, and go round the ends of the line and back to their place. The rhyme is repeated for each couple.

8 MUSICAL BUMPS

The children dance to lively music. When it stops, they sit quickly on the floor. The last to sit down are out. The music begins again, and others are eliminated.

9 MUSICAL STICK

You will need a walking-stick.

The children form a circle, with one child holding the walking-stick. When the music begins he taps the stick on the floor three times, and passes it to the next child, who does the same. When the music stops, the child left holding the stick is out. The game continues until only one child is left.

10 POISON BALL

You will need a large plastic ball.

The leader throws the ball at the children. Anyone who is touched by the poison ball joins the leader, and tries to hit other children. The last child to be touched is declared the winner.

11 POP GOES THE WEASEL

Form the children into small rings (three or four), with one child in the middle of each ring, and one child outside. The children all sing:

> Half a pound of tuppenny rice,
> Half a pound of treacle,
> That's the way the money goes,
> *Pop* goes the weasel.

On the word 'Pop' the children have to come out of the ring and find another home, while the child outside rushes to an empty ring.

12 RING-A-RING O' ROSES

The children form a circle and dance round singing

> Ring-a-ring o'roses,
> A pocket full of posies,
> A-tishoo, a-tishoo,
> We all fall down,

at which they all fall to the ground.

13 SEA AND HER CHILDREN

Divide the children into groups with leaders. One leader is the 'sea'. The different groups are given the names of fish. When called into the sea, they stand near the leader who is the 'sea'. She tells them:
    'The sea is choppy' (they jump).
    'The sea is calm' (they walk).
When she says, 'There's a storm at sea, and the sea wants her children,' the children have to run 'home' before she catches them.

14 SPINNING THE HOOP

You will need a small wooden hoop.

The leader calls out the name of one child, at the same time starting to spin the hoop. The child must run and catch the hoop before it falls to the ground.

15 STATIONS

You will need a number of bean bags.

Stations are marked by bean bags. The children run about. At a signal each child finds a 'station' to stand behind. The leader removes a bean bag each time, so that the children are gradually eliminated.

16 TREASURE CHEST

You will need a scarf, a bunch of keys, or a baby's rattle, or a ball.

The children sit round in a circle, with one child in the middle, who is blindfolded and is guarding his treasure (the rattle, etc.) The leader points his magic finger at any child in the circle. This child then creeps towards the treasure and attempts to take it without the blindfolded child hearing. If the blindfolded child hears a sound, he points towards the direction from which he thinks the sound is coming. If he points in the right direction, the moving child must sit down, and the magic finger points to someone else. If a child is successful in taking the 'treasure', he takes the place of the blindfolded person.

58

17 WHAT'S THE TIME, MR. WOLF?

The leader stands at one end of the pitch (he is Mr. Wolf), and the children at the opposite end. At a signal the children approach from their end, and Mr. Wolf from his end. The children say, 'What's the time, Mr. Wolf?' Mr. Wolf replies, 'Eight o'clock' (or any other hour). This is repeated until Mr. Wolf says 'Dinner-time'. Then he chases the children and catches all he can before they reach their 'home'. The children who have been caught join Mr. Wolf at the catching end until all the children are caught.

Variation: **SAVAGE SAM**

Children: 'What shall we bring you today, Savage Sam?'

Savage Sam: 'Knives and forks', or 'Water', or 'A cup of tea', etc. But when Savage Sam says, 'My dinner', the children flee for 'home'.

Variation: **ARE YOU READY, MR. WOLF?**

Make one side of the room 'home', and form the children into a circle round the one chosen to be Mr. Wolf. They should be just out of touching distance. Then all together the children call out, 'Are you ready, Mr. Wolf? Mr. Wolf then says something like, 'No, I've still got to put on my trousers', or, 'No, I've still got to put on my waistcoat'. Whatever item of clothing is mentioned, Mr. Wolf has to pretend to put them on. After being asked three or four times if he is ready, he might suddenly say, 'Ready now'. Then Mr. Wolf rushes for the children, and the children rush for 'home'. Whoever is caught becomes the next Mr. Wolf.

18 WIZARD

You will need a stick, or ruler.

This is a simple noisy game for the very small ones. The leader explains that he is going to be a wizard and that the stick that he holds in his hand is a magic one. With it he can turn the children into all kinds of different things. When he waves the magic wand and calls out the name of some animal, bird, or

59

thing, the children must imitate the actions of whatever is named — such as a duck, frog, aeroplane,
train, dog, sheep, clown, etc.

SECTION 6B
FINGER PLAYS

The games in this section of 'Indoor Games for Very
Young Children' are aimed at teaching children to
use their fingers and hands, and to co-ordinate them
with appropriate words. They can be used with any
number, though ideally a group of twenty or so is
sufficient.

1   HERE IS THE BEEHIVE

Here is the beehive (hold up clenched hand)
But where are the bees?
Hiding away where nobody sees.
Now they come creeping out of the hive,
One, two, three, four, five (straighten fingers
    one at a time)
And away they fly (flying movement with fin-
    gers),
Buzz, buzz, buzz, buzz, buzz.

2   OPEN, SHUT THEM

(Actions apply to both hands throughout)
Open, shut them, open, shut them, give a little
    clap,
Open, shut them, open, shut them, put them in
    your lap.
Creeping, creeping, gently creeping right up to
    your chin,
Open wide your little mouth and pop a finger in.

Falling, falling, quickly falling right down to the ground,
Pick them quickly up again, and turn them round and round.

3 SQUIRRELS

Five little squirrels sitting in a tree (hold up five fingers of right hand)
The first one said, What can I see? (indicate which finger with left hand)
The second one said, I see a gun (indicate which finger with left hand)
The third one said, Away let us run (indicate which finger with left hand)
The fourth one said, Let's hide in the shade (indicate which finger with left hand)
The fifth one said, I'm not afraid (indicate which finger with left hand)
But BANG went the gun (a loud clap)
And away they all ran (show them running away).

4 TOMMY THUMB

Having selected the right finger (or thumb), the children hide their hands behind their backs, bringing them forward with the appropriate finger upright, the remaining ones clenched.

Tommy Thumb, Tommy Thumb, where are you?
Here I am, here I am, how do you do?
Peter Pointer, Peter Pointer, where are you?
Here I am, here I am, how do you do?
Teddy Tall, Teddy Tall, where are you?
Here I am, here I am, how do you do?
Ruby Ring, Ruby Ring, where are you?
Here I am, here I am, how do you do?
Sammy Small, Sammy Small, where are you?
Here I am, here I am, how do you do?

5 TRAIN

Here is the train line, and here is the train (stretch out right arm, left hand clenched),

Chuff, chuff, chuff, along the line (place left hand in palm of right hand and move up to shoulder), And chuff, chuff, chuff back again (move back again).

SECTION 6C
ACTION AND MOVEMENT
SONGS

The games in this section of 'Indoor Games for Very Young Children' aim at helping them to co-ordinate actions with words.

1 BOUNCING BALL

I'm like a great big bouncing ball (action),
High in the air, then down I fall (action).
Now I run along the ground (action),
Now I'm turning round and round and round (action).

2 I STAMP MY FEET

Sung to the tune of *The Vicar of Bray*, with actions throughout.

I stamp my feet and wriggle my toes,
And clap my hands as the music goes.
I reach to the sky and touch the ground,
Up and down to the music's sound.
I rock to and fro the way the wind blows,
It's time to go when the music goes.
I bounce up and down like a bouncy ball,
And then I stretch and grow very tall.

3 JACK IN THE BOX

My Jack in the box jumps like this (crouch on ground, then an enormous jump),

And he makes me laugh as he wiggles his head
(action).
Then I gently press him down again (action),
Saying, Quick in the box you must go to bed (action).
My Jack in the box is a funny old man,
He sits in his box as still as he can,
He sits in his box as still as he can,
Then *suddenly* out he pops (spring up quickly),
In, out, in, out, funny old Jack in the box (up and
down),
In, out, in, out, funny old Jack in the box.

4 MISS POLLY HAD A DOLLY

*You will need a doll in a cradle, a small bag and hat
for the doctor, and a small chair beside the cradle for
Miss Polly to sit on.*

Miss Polly had a dolly who was sick, sick, sick,
So she telephoned the doctor to come quick,
quick, quick (action).
The doctor came with his bag and his hat
(action),
And he knocked upon the door with a rat-a-tat-
tat (action).
He looked at the dolly and he shook his head
(action).
He said, Miss Polly, put her straight to bed (point
finger).
He wrote a prescription for a pill, pill, pill
(action).
I'll be back in the morning with the bill, bill, bill
(wave goodbye).

5 PETER HAMMERS WITH ONE HAMMER

To the tune *The Vicar of Bray.* Words, music and
actions will be found in *Music for the Nursery
School.*

6 MOO, MOO, THIS IS WHAT THE COW SAYS*

* *Music for the Nursery School*, by Linda Chesterman, published by George G. Harrap & Co. Ltd.

† *Action Songs for Babies*, by A. W. I. Chitty, published by W. Paxton & Co. Ltd., 36–39 Dean Street, London, W.1.

SECTION 7
INDOOR GAMES
FOR JUNIORS

1 ANIMALS

This is another version of 'Blind-man's Buff'. All the players except the blind-man station themselves in different parts of the room. The blindfolded player then feels his way round the room until he touches somebody. The player who is touched must immediately make the noise of some animal – a donkey, cat, dog, cow, pig etc. repeating it three times if requested. The blind-man must guess the name of his victim by the voice. If he is successful, the person named becomes blind-man; if unsuccessful, the blind-man must release his prisoner and try again.

2 ASCOT BONNET

You will need 2 large bonnets with ribbons for tying under the chin.

The players divide into teams and stand in rows. The leader of each team puts on the bonnet – and ties the ribbons into a bow beneath his chin. Number two undoes the bow, puts on the bonnet, ties the ribbon, and so on down the line. The first team to cover every head wins.

The race can be complicated by giving each team a pair of enormous bedsocks as well. The players have to don and doff the bonnet, the leader must also put on the bedsocks, which number two takes off him and puts on himself, and so on down the line.

Shoes are removed before the game if bedsocks are included.

3 BALLOON BURSTING

You will need a balloon for each player.

Teams of even numbers stand behind a starting line, and on the command, No. 1 of each team runs to a chair at a given distance in front of each team. The object is to burst the balloon which is on the chair by sitting on it, and then return to the start. The team which finishes first is the winner.

Variation:
Each player has a balloon tied to his ankle. The object is to tread on and burst the other opponents' balloons. The last player with his balloon intact wins (not a game for stilletto heels!).

4 BALLOON CABER

You will need one balloon (and some spares are advisable) and some matchsticks.

Standing behind a line, each player tries to throw the balloon as far forwards as possible. The spot at which it touches the ground is marked by a matchstick, or a piece of card, with the thrower's initials written on it. The game can be made more amusing by the use of a sausage-shaped balloon.

5 BEACHCOMBERS

You will need a variety of simple objects such as match boxes, pieces of wool, empty cotton reels.

The players are divided into two teams. One half are 'beachcombers' the others are 'waves'. The playing area is divided by a half-way line. Two other lines, one at either end, mark the boundaries for the game. The 'waves' and 'beachcombers' line up behind their boundary lines. The items are scattered on the 'combers' half of the playing area. On the command 'Go' the 'combers' rush out and pick up the scattered treasure and take it home. At the same time the 'waves' rush forward trying to tag their opponents before they reach the safety of home. If caught the gatherer is out. The game recommences and is played till all the team is caught. The teams then reverse roles.

The game can be competitive if the objects are given numbers. The team gaining the highest total declared the winners.

6 BEAN GAME

This can be played with any number. A circle is formed. Participants rotate in a clockwise direction as names are called out by some elected person in the centre.

'Runner Beans' – All run round.
'Broad Beans' – Walk round with chests out.
'Dwarf Beans' – Walk round, crouching.
'String Beans' – Skip round holding hands.
'Haricot Beans' – Hop round.
'Baked Beans' – All scatter – anyone caught before reaching the extremity of the hall or

room are 'in the tin'. They help to catch the next time round – the last person left is the winner.

7 BILLY'S TROUSERS

The children sit in a circle with an adult in the centre, who says, 'Billy's lost his trousers', looks around and adds, 'and I think I know who's taken them – it's you!' and he points suddenly at one child. This child must not speak or smile, but must shake his head and point quickly at another child. That child in turn shakes his head and points at another player. Anyone who speaks or smiles is out. The leader then starts the game again and continues eliminating children until only one is left.

8 BIRD STATUES

This can be played with any number.

Imitating birds flapping their wings, the players prance around the room, hopping and jumping. On the command 'Stop' everyone freezes like instant statues. Anyone moving is out. Commence again until, by the process of elimination, one player remains to be declared the winner.

9 BIRTHDAY CAKE

You will need 2 lb of flour, a pudding basin, a tray, a sweet, and a knife.

Prepare the 'cake' by pressing the flour into a basin. Turn the basin upside down on to the tray, remove the basin and put a sweet on the top of the 'cake'. The children sit in a circle round the 'cake'. One by one they are chosen to cut a slice of the cake. The slices should be very thin and should be taken from all sides of the cake so that a tower is left standing. The one who in cutting the cake causes the sweet to fall must take the sweet from the flour in his mouth without using his hands.

Variation: Pass a blunt knife round, to music. When the music stops the child holding the knife cuts a slice from the cake.

10 BLOW TABLE TENNIS BALL

You will need table tennis balls and drinking straws.
2 Dining room chairs.

Teams of 4 to 6 players are placed either end of the room. A table tennis ball is placed on the centre line. A corridor of 4 feet must be indicated to mark the playing area, with a chair (goal) at each end. At the command 'Go' both teams on all fours seek to blow the table tennis ball into the opponent's goals (between the legs of the chairs).

If there are more than two teams calls to change should be made frequently. In this case the ball remains in the same position as it was on the call of 'change', the next team having the advantage of its position on the playing area. Speed in change is therefore encouraged.

11 BUCKET CRICKET

You will need two plastic buckets and a shuttlecock,
two table tennis bats.

Make a cricket pitch — any length. The plastic buckets are a substitute for wickets. The batsman stands in front of his wicket and defends it with a table tennis bat. If the bowler succeeds in getting the shuttlecock into the bucket, the batsman is out. Other rules can be introduced by the leader to suit the players' age and conditions.

12 BLACK AND BROWN MONKEYS

You will need a number of unbreakable chairs.

Chairs are scattered about the room according to the number of players. One child is 'black monkey', the rest are 'brown monkeys', the chairs are trees and safety spots. 'Black monkey' chases the brown monkeys, but they are safe when sitting on the 'trees'. All players must circulate while the music is being played, and the chase begins when it stops.

13 CHAIRS AND TINS

You will need two small chairs, four cocoa tins or yoghurt cartons, and two scarves.

Divide the children into two teams sitting in two lines. Place the chairs, inverted, at either end of the line and put two containers on the legs of each chair. Choose one child from each team to be blindfolded. These children must crawl from their own chair to their opponent's chair, take one container from the chair and return to their own chair. They put the container on the leg of their own chair, and then crawl to their opponent's chair to take another container. The child who gets all four containers on the legs of his chair is declared the winner. If the children become tired before a point has been scored, two other children can be chosen to take their place.

14 CHINESE LAUNDRY

Players will need to produce a variety of articles, such as a red tie, a left black shoe, a white cardigan, a grey sock, a scarf, a ninepenny stamp, a hairgrip, a vest.

Divide the children into four equal groups and place one group in each corner of the room. Appoint one captain for each group. The leader calls out the names of the articles that he lost when he sent his washing to the laundry. When an article is named, each team tries to find one. It is taken out (or off) and given to the team captain, who runs with it to the leader, who should be standing in the middle of the room. The first team to reach the leader wins the point.

15 CIRCULAR PILLAR BALL

You will need two balls.

This game caters for reasonably large numbers and may be played in a small space. The players arrange themselves as shown in the diagram. The attackers, stationed around the circle, endeavour to hit the post; the defenders try to prevent the post being hit. The ball must be passed by hand and not held for more than two seconds. Each group of defenders, when in possession of the ball, should endeavour to pass it to their own attackers in the opposite half of the circle, but all groups are restricted to their own playing area. Two balls can be used if desired. Each hit on the target scores two points. If a defender should accidentally knock down the post, the opposing side is credited with one point.

16 CRACKER WHISTLE

You will need dry biscuits, paper plates and whistles for each team.
Any number of teams can take part in this competition.

Place 2 or 3 biscuits on plates about 1.5 metres apart on a line in front of the team. On the signal 'Go', the first player in the team runs to the first plate. Eating the biscuits he then blows a whistle, as soon as he is able. He runs back to his team handing the whistle to the next player. The game continues until all players have eaten their biscuits and made a blast on the whistle and are safely back at the commencement line.

17 COCK FIGHT

Players in a circle are numbered. One is chosen to be 'King Cock'. The leader calls a number to seek to dethrone the 'King'. Both squat and hold their ankles. They hop and bump trying to make their opponent topple over or let go of his ankles. The winner is then challenged by another. This is a survival of the fittest!

18 DEAD SOLDIERS

This is a good game to restore quietness after a noisy game. The children lie in a comfortable position on the floor. The object is that they should lie *still*. As soon as a child moves he is out. The last child left in is the winner.

19 DOTTO

You will need six sketches of famous faces on large sheets of paper (these can be traced from the newspaper, using an enlarging device).

The drawings should be reduced to about thirty dots, erasing the outlines, so that if the dots are joined up the drawing appears. These dots should be numbered from 1 to 30. Thirty questions are prepared, and each time one is answered correctly another dot is joined up. Any player may at any time make a guess as to the identity of the subject, but an incorrect guess eliminates the player.

20 DOWN WITH THE PIN

You will need a skittle, 2 balls placed in a box at an equal distance from the skittle and in the centre of two teams who stand on either side.

Players in both teams are numbered. When their number is called, the players run to their ball, stand behind the container, then throw until one of them knocks down the pin. Points are scored for the team.

21 FARMYARD FROLIC

Players divide into teams of three, four or five, one of whom is leader and the others animals of their own choosing. Scatter about the venue a large number of buttons or Smarties or indigestion tablets, and set the team members on to searching for the objects, leaving the team leader sitting on the chair. When the team members find one of the objects they make a noise like their chosen animal until their leader comes to collect it. After, say ten minutes, the team whose leader has the most objects, wins. An extra prize can be awarded to the team making the most original and life-like animal noises.

22 FARMYARD

You will need sufficient pieces of paper for each child to receive one on which have been written the names of different animals. Each name should be repeated four times.

Give out the pieces of paper folded. On the signal the children look at them, and begin to move around, making the noise of their animal, e.g. cat, lion, pig. The children making the noise of the same animal collect together in a family. The last family to find all its four members is eliminated and their papers are confiscated. The papers from the other groups are collected in and re-distributed amongst the remaining players. The game is repeated until only one group is left.

23 FREE THREE SHIES

You will need containers of all kinds. Discarded men's or women's socks rolled into small bundles for throwing. A table or box.

Mark the containers with numbers from 1–6, smaller items having larger numbers. Line-up on a table and place a line 3–4 metres away from the table. Players in turn try to knock the tins off the table or box scoring the number on the tin or container. A good knock-out competition or team game.

24 FRONT AND BACK RACES

You will need two saucers, and a dozen buttons, beans, shells, or similar small objects per team.

Teams of equal numbers stand sideways in line. On the floor, by the leader of each team are two saucers or similar receptacles, one containing the twelve (more if desired and available) small objects, the other empty. On the starting signal, the leader picks up one object at a time and passes it to the second in the team, who passes it to the third, and so on down the line. When the object reaches the last player he begins to pass it back down the line behind his back; thus, at the same time some objects are being passed in one direction in front of the body and in the other direction behind the body. When the leader receives the objects behind his back he puts them into the second and previously empty saucer. He must also count them as they come back to him, so that the instant he knows that the last object has come back and been placed in the saucer, he can shout 'Up', to indicate that his team has completed the race. The number of objects to be passed can be varied at will, but whenever possible it should be at least twice the number of players in the team, so that automatically every player will be involved, at some period, in passing objects in both directions at the same time. The race should be run not less than four times, starting from one end on two occasions, and from the opposite end for the remaining two races.

25 GET THAT SEAT

You will need as many chairs as there are players placed in a circle in the middle of the room.
All players except one seat themselves.

One chair remains vacant, and the game is for the player who is 'out' to try to sit down on the vacant chair while the others try to prevent his doing so by moving first in one direction and then in another.

If the players move from chair to chair quickly the player who is out has any amount of trouble before he can secure a seat. When he does succeed, the player sitting on the chair to his right takes his place.

26 HAND FOOTBALL

You will need a large rubber ball, or football (though a small ball can be used), two skittles or tins.

The court is marked as shown in diagram. The goal-posts can be drawn with chalk, or marked by two skittles, or tins, or similar objects. All dimensions indicated in the diagram can be changed if so desired, and are largely dependent upon the playing area available. Similarly, the rules given below are for guidance only. They may be changed or modified to suit local conditions. It is suggested, however, that they should be kept as simple as possible.

(1) The object of the game is to score goals.

(2) The ball is propelled or knocked by the open hand or fist along the ground and must always be kept below knee height.

(3) A ball which passes through the goal higher than knee height does not count as a goal.

27 HAT LEAP-FROG

You will need a cap or hat for each player.

One person makes a back for leap-frog – feet fairly wide apart. Each competitor leaps over, straddle leg, and then places his hat on the back. The pile grows higher and more difficult. When some one knocks the pile over he is counted out. Recommence the game, gradually eliminating the group until the winner remains.

28 HENS AND FOXES

Object, to gain a larger family. The game can become quite boisterous with older children.

One player represents a fox, the other a hen with a large brood of chicks. The fox is hungry, and is anxious to get one of the chicks for his supper, but the hen makes a desperate effort to protect her brood, who cluster behind her in a long 'tail' each holding the one in front by the waist. The determined fox tries to snatch a chick, the hen puts up a hard fight. Facing the fox, her frightened brood sway from side to side with every movement of her outspread wings (arms). If the fox successfully grabs the last chick on the tail the victim joins the fox (holding his waist). If the hen can catch the tail of the fox it joins on the hen's tail. The game goes on with the hen and fox each trying to gain more chicks for their 'tails'. After a suitable length of time the one with the longest tail wins.

29 HIDDEN HALVES

You will need a number of pieces of cardboard bearing the names of different towns, and cut in half.

When there are children of all ages at a party this is a game which can be adapted to suit the different age-groups. The slips containing the second parts of the words should be hidden over the room or house, and the children given the first halves. They must find the letters which will complete their half of a town. For younger children the words can be split simply, so that they are easy to read – for instance, LON and DON instead of LO and NDON. Or the older ones can be given the second half of the word, and have to hunt for the first half. The game can be played with the names of flowers, advertising slogans, proverbs – there are many variations. As soon as a player has completed his town, he takes both halves to the leader, who gives him another half. The child to complete the most towns in a given time is the winner.

30 HIDDEN TREASURE

You will need a ball of string or wool for each child.

The string, or wool, is wound round and round the room, under furniture, round knobs, crossing and recrossing the other balls. At the end of each string there is a prize, or all ends can be tied to the same parcel containing a prize for the first child there. When there are various ages individual prizes are better. The children are given one end of the string, and told to follow the trail, winding up as they go, to the 'hidden treasure'.

31 HUMAN NOUGHTS AND CROSSES

You will need nine chairs.

Two teams, one 'Noughts' and the other 'Crosses', with nine chairs set out in rows of three. The leader calls out 'Nought' and 'Cross' alternately, and members of the teams go in turn and sit on the chairs, the object being to get a row of three human 'Noughts' or 'Crosses', exactly as in the paper game. The side that gets a row of three takes a point – a draw counts to neither side. When each game is over those who have played go to the end of their team, so that everyone is given a chance to play. As the team to take up the first position has the advantage, if a 'Nought' has been called first on the first round, a 'Cross' should be called first on the second round.

32 HUNT THE WHAT-NOTS

You will need a bag and five articles for each team.

A volunteer representing his team is blindfolded for each round. The bag is left with his team, the swag, 5 items, say from the kitchen, are placed at the other end of the playing area. The volunteers, on the word 'Go' move forward directed by their team towards the booty. They have to find and then bring back to the bag, which is with the team, each item individually. Amid all the noise, the confusion and bumping into other blindfolded volunteers, the items are retrieved. The team securing their articles in their swag bag first is the winner.

33   IN THE DARK

You will need scarves for blindfolds and a small hand bell.

All the players are blindfolded except one, whom it is their object to catch. The unblindfolded player carries with him a little bell which tinkles with every movement of his body, revealing his whereabouts to the other players, who are all making frantic efforts to catch him. Make sure this is well supervised if there are obstacles – furniture etc. which could prove hazardous.

34   JUMPING FROGS

You will need for each player a flat cardboard frog with a piece of string threaded through it.

One end of the string is tied to a chair on the opposite side of the room, and the child holds the other end. By wiggling their strings to make the frogs jump, the children race their frogs to the end of the string. At a large party this race can be run off in heats.

35   KNIGHTS' COMBAT

Definitely a rough game, but lads love it! Boys in pairs, one riding 'piggy-back'. He's the knight on his horse. The combat between two pairs is won when one knight is tumbled to the floor or dismounted.

The winning pair can challenge others or the game can be played as a team game.

36   MAZARATTI

You will need two scarves, a rug, and two newspapers rolled into two long sticks.

Two people are blindfolded, and lie on the rug in the middle of the floor, holding each other by the left hand, with the sticks in their right hands. One player asks, 'Are you there, Mazaratti?' The other player replies 'Yes'. The first player then attempts to strike the second player on his head with the newspaper stick. The players must continue to hold hands, and they must keep their shoulders on the floor, but they are at liberty to dodge. They take it in turn to ask the question, and then strike. When one player has struck the other on his head he is declared the winner, and a new couple are chosen.

Variation: **GLADIATORS**

Two 'gladiators' are chosen, blindfolded, and 'armed' with a newspaper stick. They stalk each other until one lands a blow on the other, and is acclaimed the champion, at which point another contender is pushed into the ring.

37 MUSICAL BEAN BAGS

You will need enough bean bags or similar objects for each competitor, less one.

Bags are placed in the centre. When music begins players run round in a clockwise direction. When music stops they rush into centre and grab a bag. The unfortunate competitor who fails to get a bag sits for the rest of the game on the edge of the circle— one or more bean bags are removed each time.

38 MUSICAL CHAIRS

You will need one chair to each player.

The chairs should be arranged in two lines, back to back, with the children sitting on them. When the music begins the children get up and walk in a clockwise direction. The leader removes at least one chair. When the music stops the children sit on the nearest chair. They must not move in an anti-clockwise direction, even if there is a chair just behind them. Any child not finding a chair is out.

39 MUSICAL CHAOS

You will need one chair to each player.

This game is like Musical Chairs, but more exuberant. The chairs are arranged in a circle (facing inwards), and instead of marching round, the children charge about inside the circle until the music stops.

40 MUSICAL LAPS

You will need enough chairs for half the number of players.

This game is played on the same principal as Musical Chairs, except that half the children remain seated, and the rest have to find a lap to sit on instead of a chair when the music stops.

41 MUSICAL MATS

You will need a piece of newspaper per player.

Pieces of newspaper are placed on the ground. When the music stops, the last child to step on the 'mat' is out. The pieces of paper are removed one by one as the children are eliminated.

42 MUSICAL NUMBERS

The children walk round the room as the music is being played. When the music stops the leader calls out a number, e.g. seven. The children move into groups of seven. Children who are not collected into groups of the correct number are eliminated. The game is repeated until two children are left, who are the winners.

43 MUSICAL STATUES

The children run around while the music is played; when it stops they stand quite still; if anyone moves he is out.

44 NURSERY RHYMES

A number of teams compete to see which can think up (and sing in turn) the largest number of different nursery rhymes.

45 ORCHESTRA

One child is sent out of the room, the others sit in a circle. A 'Conductor' is appointed who pretends to play an instrument (say, the violin), while all sing a well-known tune. The exile returns, and has to guess who is the 'Conductor', while the 'Conductor' must change frequently from one 'instrument' to another (e.g. drum, flute, trombone), all the others following his lead.

46 ONE LEG PULL

This is similar to a Tug of War except that players are only allowed to stand on one leg. Anyone infringing this law is counted out.

47 PASSING THE COINS

You will need two 2p pieces.

Two teams face each other in lines, with arms outstretched and fists clenched. A penny is placed on the back of the hand of both the end players. On the command 'Go', the players slide the penny from one hand to the other, and then on to the nearer hand of the next player, and so on up the line. The penny must pass to the end without dropping. Should it fall, it is returned to the leader and the process set in motion again. The team completing the transfer in the approved manner is the winner.

Variations: Other objects, such as sugar cubes, sweets or chocolates, can be used in place of coins. Similar passing games can be devised, e.g. passing tennis balls from chin to chin, sugar cubes by each participant having a teaspoon held in the mouth or in the hand, match-boxes on the end of the nose. (Editorial comment: Most unhygienic!).

48 PATTERNS

The children arrange themselves into teams of six or eight. When the music starts they walk about quite freely. As they are walking the leader calls out a letter or shape, say, a square, or the letter E. The moment the music stops, each team rushes to form the shape, or letter, called out. The team that makes the best shape within ten seconds is awarded a point.

49 PIRATES

You will need seven stones, or seven shoes, or other small objects.

The children are divided into four equal groups, with one group sitting in each corner. The seven stones are put in the centre of the room, with a square drawn around them, and a small square in front of each team. Each team member is given a number, from 1 onwards. The leader calls out a number, e.g. 8; the four people whose number is 8 run to the centre of the room and pick up a stone, bringing it to their own square. Only one stone can be picked up at a time. It must be placed in the square, and not thrown. They then return to the centre and pick up another stone, which must be placed in the same square, and not thrown. They then return to the centre and pick up another stone. When all the stones have been picked up from the centre, the Number 8s then take the stones from their opponents' squares. This continues until one of the 'pirates' has three stones in his square. This 'pirate' gains a point for his team. The leader then calls out other numbers, and the team with the most points wins.

50 PUSS IN THE CORNER

One player, who is 'Puss', stands in the middle of the room, while the others each take a corner. No player must keep possession of his or her corner for more than twenty seconds at a time. The game begins by one of the players beckoning to another to change places. While they are changing, Puss makes a rush for one of the unoccupied corners. If she succeeds in getting to the corner first, the player who is left out takes her place in the middle and the next round commences.

51 PENALTY KNOCKOUT

You will need one tennis or similar ball.

Players in a circle throw the ball to each other. Anyone dropping a catch is progressively penalized.

First Fault – Kneels on one knee but catches with both hands.

Second Fault – On both knees but uses two hands.

Third Fault – On both knees, catching with only right hand.

Fourth Fault – Kneels on both knees and uses only left hand.

Fifth Fault – He's out!

Each time a player who is paying a penalty catches a ball he regains one place.

A fascinating but time consuming game.

52 PIGGY IN THE MIDDLE

You will need one ball, preferably a frido football.

Two players stand as far apart as desired and a third player stands in the middle. The two players on the outside throw the ball at each other while the third tries to intercept. If he succeeds he changes place with the thrower and becomes – 'Piggy'.

53 POSING

Divide players into two or more teams.

The leader announces that he is a film director in need of characters for his crowd scenes. He may call for animals or people.

Using an adjective he describes a pose which he requires. For example – 'Kneeling Camels', 'Swinging Monkeys' or 'Saluting Soldiers'. Characters must immediately freeze in that position or with relevant expression.

The team which freezes first is awarded points. Alternatively a panel of judges can choose the best individual pose or the most realistic looking team.

Some ideas for posing.
The most ridiculous clown.
The most frightening sergeant.
The saddest snail.
The most spectacular goal-keeper.
The most humorous smiler.
The most merry reveller.
The most convincing politician.

54 RING THAT BELL

You will need a hand bell or box with peas which rattle and a blindfold.

A player stands in the centre of a circle; feet astride with the bell on the floor between his feet. Blind-folded he has to listen for the approach of any player who gets a sign from the leader. Stealthily the intruder moves towards the bell. If the blindfolded guard of the treasure points directly at the approaching thief, the robber is out or changes places. If the robber can reach and ring the bell, without being detected, he gains an individual point.

It is best to set a time limit for each 'robbing' e.g. 30 seconds to 45 seconds. This speeds up the operation and saves other players from being bored through inactivity.

55 SALE BARGAINS

Four corners or areas are designated as shops, e.g. Toy shop, Chemist, Grocer, Greengrocer. All players assemble in the middle of the room. The leader calls a commodity found in one of the shops – players rush to the shop. The last person to reach the shop is out. Players who go to the wrong shop are also counted out.

The winner of the last round, in which there will be two remaining competitors, is the person reaching the correct designation first.

56 SHIPWRECK

You will need labels for parts of a ship.

Various parts of the room are labelled as parts of a ship (e.g. deck, lifeboat, bridge, captain's cabin, etc.). The children march round the middle of the room until there is a shout of 'On deck!' or 'To the lifeboats!' The last one arriving in the correct zone is out – presumably drowned.

57 SHOPPING

You will need four 'shops' each bearing a placard telling of a selection of wares, and slips of paper with names of commodities, and some counters or beans.

Four 'shops' are set up, each bearing a placard displaying its wares (e.g. butter, toys, shoes). Each child is given a slip of paper with a commodity named on it (say, a pair of shoes), and must take it to the correct shop, receiving in exchange for it a counter or a bean. On showing this to the leader he is given another slip of paper, and so on. The winner is the one with the most counters at the end of the game. Another, simpler, version involves all the children marching round to music. When the music stops the leader shouts out a commodity, and the children have to run to the correct shop (e.g. the butchers for meat, or the dairy for milk). Any going to the wrong shop are 'out'.

58 SHOUTING SHOPS

While one child is out of the room the others decide on what kind of shop they are going to have. Then each child chooses the name of an article which is sold in that shop – for instance, if a grocer's shop is decided on, then they can choose things like butter, bacon, sugar, tea, biscuits, etc. The child outside is then allowed in, and immediately all the others start shouting out the names of the articles they have chosen. The child from outside has to guess what kind of shop the other children have chosen.

59 STORY TIME

A story is told, and everyone present is allocated a character or object in it (e.g. Robin Hood, Friar Tuck, the sheriff, the sheriff's horse, the river, the town walls, and so on). Every time their character or object is mentioned they stand up, spin round, and sit down again. On the mention of some all-inclusive object (perhaps 'the Merry Men') everybody has to stand up and spin round.

60 TAG THE SNAKE'S TAIL

Two teams in two lines. Players make a team snake by holding the waist of the person in front. On the command 'Go' the leader of each team tries to catch the tail of the opponent. When caught the last player drops out. The game comes to an end when only one player is left – the other team has obviously won.

61 TIMED WALKING

You will need a watch with an easy to read second hand.

Competitors at one end of the room line up across the room. On command 'Go' they have to walk over a measured distance to the other end in the time stated. It could be 30 seconds or whatever the time keeper stipulates. Anyone reaching the finishing line before time is up is disqualified. The winner is the one who gets home nearest to the correct timing.

62 TRAMPS' TEA-PARTY

You will need a knife, fork, scarf, gloves, old hat, a dice, parcel wrapped in newspaper, a bar of chocolate being in the middle.

The children sit in a large circle with the parcel in the centre of the room on a table or on the floor. Each child throws the dice in turn. When a six is thrown the thrower goes to the parcel, puts on the clothes, and begins undoing the parcel, using the knife and fork. As soon as another player throws a six, he takes the clothes off the first player, puts them on himself, and proceeds to continue unwrapping the parcel. When the bar of chocolate is unwrapped, the player who is the winner eats the chocolate, using the knife and fork.

63   TUNNEL BALL

You will need one ball for each team.

The children are divided into equal teams, e.g. four teams of ten children, and stand in a straight line one behind the other, with their legs astride. On the signal the first child rolls the ball along the ground through the tunnel made by the legs of the team. The last child in the team picks up the ball and runs to the front of the team. He then rolls the ball down the tunnel. The game continues until the leader is standing at the front of his team, all the children having had a turn at rolling the ball.

Variations: The ball can be passed above the heads of the team instead of through the tunnel, or alternately over the head and through the legs, so that the first person passes the ball to the person behind him by throwing it over his head; the second person catches it and passes it backwards by throwing it under his legs. Another variation is that the children can crawl through the tunnel instead of using a ball. As soon as the first person has reached the back, the second person can begin crawling. The team must move forward as each person reaches the back, unless there is unlimited space.

Another variation is to have the players at the start in line side by side on 'all fours'. They raise their seats to form a tunnel, through which players crawl in quick succession. Or, players can lie face down, from which position they raise their seats to form a tunnel. This is suitable only for older and stronger players.

64 TWO DOGS, ONE BONE

You will need a pair of socks rolled into a ball (the 'bone').

The players are divided into two equal teams, who sit on chairs in line facing each other, at least 6 to 8 feet apart. They then number off down the line, starting at the right-hand side of each team. Midway between the two teams, on the floor, is placed the 'bone'. The leader stands at one end of, and midway between, the two lines. He then calls out any number, say 'Two'. Number Two from each team then dashes out and tries to grab the 'bone'.

65 TWO AND FIVE PENCE

You will need one bucket of water and some 5p pieces plus 6 × 2p pieces for each child.

Five or six children gather around the bucket in which a 5p piece is seen at the bottom. Each contestant takes turn in dropping a 2p piece into the water endeavouring to cover the silver coin. The first player to completely cover the target is the winner. If you feel generous, he keeps both coins!

66 WASHING DAY

You will need lengths of cord, pegs and clothes.

Divide into teams. Using one hand only each player has to peg one or more garments on a clothes line with two pegs for each garment. The fun is encouraged as on the word 'Go' a scramble is made to the line. The first team to complete hanging the washing and be back squatting on the floor are winners.

67 WINDING STRING

You will need two balls of string.

Two teams of even numbers stand facing each other about 5 feet apart. On the word 'Go' the first player of each row gives the end of the string to player No. 2. Then No. 1 holds the ball while No. 2 winds it up, using the end handed to him. As soon as No. 2 has finished the winding, he grips the complete ball and hands the end to No. 3, whose turn it now is to wind up. The game proceeds in this pattern. The speed, plus the knotting mistakes, make this good entertainment.

SECTION 8
INDOOR GAMES
FOR TEENAGERS

1 AGILITY

You will need one chair and one matchbox.

This is an amusing test of agility that will appeal to boys. Place a matchbox on end behind the right-hand rear leg of a wooden chair. The object is for the player to pick this up in his teeth while remaining on the chair. If any part of the body touches the ground the attempt has failed. It is a possible, but very difficult, feat.

2 ARE YOU?

You will need to prepare a list of famous couples before the event: Paul & Barnabas, Anthony & Cleopatra, Dan & Doris Archer and so on.

Write each name on a separate slip of paper which is folded in half and placed in a box and shuffled.

Players sit in a ring, and each is handed a name which he keeps hidden from the others. Then each player in turn is allowed to ask one question of anyone in the circle, trying to identify his partner. He must not ask a direct question however, such as: 'Are you Cleopatra?' until he is fairly certain of the player's identity. The first to challenge correctly is the winner, and he and his partner drop out of the ring. The game continues until only two are left, and they are awarded a booby prize.

3 ART GALLERY

You will need a pile of old newspapers.

At the beginning of the game, newspapers are distributed to everyone — no teams this time, and no need for the same edition. The leader then calls out an object, a bunch of bananas, a string of sausages, a horse, a spade, a church building etc. — and the players have to tear out the appropriate shape. The game is continued for several items, and an 'art gallery' of exhibits arranged at the end. The player producing the best array is awarded a small prize.

4 ASSOCIATED NUMBERS

Players sit facing M.C. who calls out a number and points to a player. The selected player must immediately respond by shouting back an associated word or phrase. Failure to respond is counted as a black mark — three black marks and the player is out.

Examples of associations:

Number	Association
4	Seasons or Gospels.
10	Commandments.
2	is company three is not.

5 AUNT AGATHA'S AGONY COLUMN

You will need pencils and paper for each player.

Everyone is given a small paper and pencil. Each player silently and without comment writes a problem or dilemma in one sentence (e.g. If I had my toe stuck in a lift door ...... If my nose got caught in a sausage machine ...... If my wig fell off.) Fold the papers and pass to someone of the opposite sex or another team. They have to write a solution without looking at the problem. The leader selects the best and reads them later to the players. Hilarity is usually the result.

6 BALBY SHOW

You will need as many blank catalogues and pencils as there are players.

With invitations the hostess asks each one of her guests to bring the very earliest photo of themselves that he or she possesses. Each photograph must have the name of the original written on the back. All the pictures are arranged upon a table, placing each one upon a miniature draped easel. A numbered ticket is fixed onto each, and the exhibition is complete.

Each player is provided with a numbered catalogue and a pencil, and invited to inspect the pictures and guess the names of the originals. The guesses must be written against the corresponding numbers on the catalogue. The prettiest picture of a baby is decided by vote, each player writing his or her vote on the catalogue. Signatures are then added, the players exchange catalogues, the pictures are turned with their faces to the wall so that the names written on the back are clearly visible, and the catalogues are corrected.

The honours of the game are divided between the player who has guessed the most babies correctly, and the original of the prettiest baby picture.

7 BALANCING

You will need cotton reels, a good number!

The competitive feature of this game is to see who can balance the greatest number of reels, one on top of the other, on the back of the hand. Set a time limit.

8 BALLOON CAPERS

You will need some string and newspapers

All the boys standing at one end of the room tie balloons onto their backs, suspended in the region of their 'sit-me-down'. Girls form two parallel lines about 3 feet apart. On the word 'Go' boys start running through the female corridor while the girls attempt to burst the balloons with rolled newspapers. Boys continue to run the gauntlet until only one or two remain. These are judged the winners.

9 BALLOON CRACKERS

You will need a quantity of balloons, paper, and some small prizes.

Place numbers on tiny slips of paper inside the balloons before they are inflated. Hang them up in such a manner that they can be released together.

During the party players are told about the numbers in the balloons and that some are worth prizes. On releasing the balloons the crowd surge forward as the balloons float down from above. Much fun results as players seek to break balloons and retrieve numbers.

10 BALLOON ON THE RAILS

You will need balloons, string, several curtain rings and cream crackers!

As many string lines as there are teams are stretched between chairs; on each line hangs a balloon secured to a curtain ring. Competitors in teams have to blow the balloon from one end of their line to the other. The handicap — each competitor has to eat two cream crackers before blowing the balloon! This can be organized as a relay race, the number of lines depending on the number of players.

11 BALLOONS AND BISCUITS

You will need one balloon, one chair, one cream cracker biscuit per player.

Six players are chosen and seated in front of the audience. Each player is given a biscuit and a balloon. On a signal they eat their biscuits and then blow up their balloons until they burst. The first player to burst his balloon is the winner. A player attempting to burst his balloon in any other way must be disqualified.

Variation: The players are blindfolded, and giant-size balloons used.

12 BALLOONS IN THE BUCKET

You will need two balloons, two rolled-up news-papers and two boxes.

Two teams stand opposite each other. Balloon and paper are given to No. 1, who has to take the balloon around the length of the team, hitting it with the rolled-up paper and back into the box, which is placed at the head of the team (one hand only to be used).

13 BALLOON TENNIS

You will need two or three balloons.

Two teams stand, or better, sit facing each other. The balloon is introduced between them. The object of the game is to score goals by patting the balloon over the opposite team's heads so that it lands on the floor behind them. If it is a long team, two or three balloons can be kept going at once. If the players are seated, they must not stand to hit the balloon.

14 BISHOP'S RIDDLE

You will need small cards or papers with the individual clues, numbered, and paper and pencil for each player. Alternatively the clues can all be put together on a duplicated sheet.

Clues are put up around the room. Players are given a time limit to solve the riddles.

A bishop's riddle

1. I have a trunk
2. it has two lids
3. and two caps
4. two musical instruments
5. two established measures
6. a great number of articles carpenters can't do without

7. I always have about me two good fish
8. a great number of small shell-fish
9. two lofty trees
10. some fine flowers
11. two playful domestic animals
12. a great number of small wild animals
13. a fine stag
14. a number of whips without handles
15. some weapons of warfare
16. a number of weathercocks
17. an entrance to an hotel
18. at a political meeting on the verge of a division
19. two students
20. a number of Spanish grandees
21. a big wooden box
22. two fine buildings
23. product of camphor trees
24. a piece of old English money
25. an article used by artists
26. one used in racing
27. what is used in crossing a river
28. pair of blades without handles
29. twelfth letter of alphabet finished with bow
30. instruments used in church music

Answers.
1. My body
2. Eye
3. Kneecaps
4. Eardrums
5. Feet
6. Nails
7. Soles
8. Mussels
9. Palms
10. Tulips
11. Calves
12. Hairs
13. Heart
14. Lashes
15. Arms
16. Veins
17. Instep
18. Eyes and nose
19. Pupils
20. Tendons
21. Chest
22. Temples
23. Gums
24. Crown
25. Palate
26. Skull
27. Bridge (of nose)
28. Shoulders
29. Elbow
30. Organs

This game is attributed to an Oxford Bishop – possibly Bishop Wilberforce.

15 BLENKINSOPP-JONES

You will need several lists of imaginary firms.

To get everybody 'mixed up' and make strangers feel at home, introduce them to Blenkinsopp-Jones. The names of the imaginary firms could be: Batterby Collaro, Jenkinson Ltd., Rattlesnake, Bottomley & Throgmorton, and so on, but include at the end of *every* firm the name 'Blenkinsopp-Jones'. Each person is given a slip of paper bearing the names of his firm's directors, with *one* of them underlined. He then has to track down his 'business associates', which he will do fairly easily, except for Blenkinsopp-Jones. This is because the person who is playing the role of Blenkinsopp-Jones denies his identity until someone notices a tiny star against Blenkinsopp-Jones' name, and on the back of the paper this, in equally tiny letters: *Always known as 'Charlie'. This person, on accosting Blenkinsopp-Jones as 'Charlie', will get an affirmative reply, and, of course, has won.

16 BLIND FEEDING

You will need a table, two chairs, two tablespoons, two soup plates, two large handkerchiefs, a fair quantity of custard, porridge, or jelly, or, best of all, a mixture of all three, and two scarves.

The leader arranges the table and players so that they sit facing each other across the narrow part of the table, and so that the audience has a side view across the table. The players are blindfolded, after which a plate of food is set before each one and a large handkerchief tucked into their necks. They proceed to feed each other by filling their own spoon with the food and aiming it at the mouth of the other player, which should be kept wide open. Players should be warned against waving their spoons about wildly during play, as this can result in broken teeth. The length of the game is determined by the leader. This game is at its best when the rival players know each other very well indeed.

17 BLINDFOLDED WIRELESS

You will need two chairs and two scarves.

Two players are blindfolded and each selects a guide from the remaining company. Two chairs are placed 18 inches apart close to one corner of the room, and anything likely to cause the blindfolded players to fall is cleared away. The sightless players are stood as far from the chairs as the room allows, and non-players, including the guides, are kept well out of the way. The start being made, the guide does his best to pilot his blindfolded companion through the opening between the chairs before the opposing player reaches it. This he does by calling out suggestions, such as 'A pace to the front', 'A short turn to the right', 'Two steps to the left', and so on.

Variation: The game can be played in pairs, one player being the missile and the other the control. The missiles are blindfolded, and a mystery object is suspended in a corner of the room (a sticky bun will do). At least six missiles are set off and guided towards it with vocal instructions only by their controls. The confusion is endless, the noise deafening. Someone gets there in the end, and he is the winner.

18 BOOK REVIEWS

You will need paper and pencil for each player.

This game is run on the pattern of Consequences, the leader giving the players directions as the game proceeds. It is suitable for ten or more players. Each player begins by writing at the head of his piece of paper a real or preferably imaginary book title. He then folds the paper over so that his writing cannot be seen, and passes it to his right-hand neighbour. When all the papers have moved round one place, each player thinks of, or invents, the name of a sub-title, and writes this as near to the top of the paper as possible, though not on the fold. He then folds this over, and passes the paper on. The papers rotate until the following other items have been written on each of them:

(1) The name of the author (real or imaginary).
(2) A brief extract from the book (this should be limited to a stated number of words or lines).
(3) Another brief extract from the book.
(4) A paper in which a review appeared.
(5) What the review said.
(6) Another paper in which a review appeared.
(7) What that review said.
(8) The name of the person who bought the first copy.
(9) What he or she did with it.

When all the items have been written down (eleven in all), the papers then pass on one or more places, then each player unfolds the paper in his possession, and reads in turn what is in front of him. Alternatively the leader can read all the contributions. The papers should read as follows:

' "..." or "...", by ... Here is one extract ... Here is another extract ... The ... said "..." The ... said "..." ... bought the first copy, and ...'

19 BOSSES AND SECRETARIES

You will need a number of cuttings from newspapers, and pencils and paper.

Four to eight players on each side. The 'bosses' are given cuttings from a daily newspaper (all of equal length). The 'secretaries' have pencil and paper. The bosses stand about 12 feet away from the secretaries, facing their partner (if space allows). The boss then dictates the contents of the newspaper-cutting to his secretary, who takes it down. The first pair with a complete record of dictation are the winners.

Variation: Put a large sweet in the mouth of the 'boss' before he starts to dictate.

20 BOWLS BONANZA

*You will need 12 empty washing-up liquid contain-
ers per game plus one tennis ball. Match-boxes or
Smartie packets can be used instead of plastic containers.*

The 'Pins' are set out in a triangular pattern. Teams
of 3 to 5 people are selected. Draw a 'start' line. Each
person is allowed two shots at the 'Pins'. The team
scores one point per knock-down pin, the team with
the highest aggregate total is the winner.

21 BUDDING POETS

You will need paper and a pencil for each player.

Players sit in a ring, and each writes three lines of
poetry at the top of his paper: the first two lines
making a rhyming couplet, the third a line which
does not rhyme with those above. He folds the
paper so that only the last line shows, and passes it
to the player on his left, who writes a line to rhyme
with the one above, completing a new couplet, and
then another line which does not rhyme. He folds
the paper so that only the last line shows. The papers are passed round thus, with two lines added
each time, until the end of the game, when each
player writes three lines to complete the poem. The
papers are then unfolded and each poem is read
aloud.

The volume of applause could indicate the winner.

22 BUZZ

The players sit in a circle. At the signal the first
person says 'One', the next says 'Two', the next
'Three', and so on. But, and this is where the catch
comes in, no seven or multiple of seven may be
mentioned at any price. Instead, the person whose
turn it is must say 'Buzz'. Thus the players must keep
an eye on 7, 14, 21, 28, etc., and also on 17, 27, 37,
etc. Any player who makes two mistakes must drop
out. The game is to see who can remain in and be the

last survivor. When a player makes a mistake the next person starts at 'One'.

23 CAMOUFLAGE

You will need about twenty small objects, and lists of them for the players.

The objects should be placed in a room so that they are in full view, but difficult to see. For example, a piece of black wool tied round the poker; a red stamp on red curtains; cellophane tape on glass; a rubber band round a chair leg, and so on. A list should be kept of where objects have been placed. Each player is given a list of the objects he has to find, with space opposite so that he can write down where he has seen each one. None of the 'hidden' objects must be removed, and it should be stressed that there is no need to move anything in the room, as all the objects are in full view. About half-an-hour can be allowed for the search.

24 CAR NAMES

You will need paper and pencil for each player.

Each sentence suggests a car name – definitely a game for the car enthusiast.

A time limit is set. The winner is the person with the highest number of correct answers.

For the uninitiated the sentences separate from the answers can be displayed with players joining them appropriately.

1. A jungle animal
2. Indian complaining about the sun
3. What does the lady say to her dog called Ronald
4. What doesn't need an engine
5. A flower
6. Cowboys greeting
7. Good name for a dog
8. One on whom you can depend

1. Jaguar
2. Dat Sun!
3. Citroen (sit Ron!)
4. Rolls
5. Daf or Lotus
6. Audi
7. Rover
8. Reliant

9. Victory	9. Triumph
10. Made to make your mouth water	10. Opel (Fruit)
11. Both from the home of H.P. Sauce	11. Aston
12. A young horse	12. Colt
13. West Coast port	13. Bristol
14. He comes from high places	14. Hillman
15. Do you smell!	15. Peugeot (Phew Jo!)

25 CHAIN

The first player calls out the name of a town, say, 'Oxford', and the next player must call out another town which begins with the last letter of the first town – in this case it would be 'd', so, for instance, 'Doncaster' could be said. The third player must then give a town beginning with 'r', for instance, 'Rotterdam'. The game continues, with players who fail to give a town or who repeat a name losing a life. When three lives have been lost, a player must drop out of the game.

26 CHANGING PLACES

You will need one chair per person. The M.C. also requires two helpers to move chairs as game proceeds.

The chairs are arranged in a circle, facing inwards, with one player sitting on each chair.

The object of the game is to whittle down the number of players and this is achieved by the following procedure:

The M.C. calls for certain players to move, e.g. 'all those wearing blue change places'. While the players are moving, the two helpers remove one or two chairs, according to the number of participants. This is similar to musical chairs. A list must be prepared beforehand, so that this game is kept moving at a reasonable pace.

Some further requests could be, 'those wearing red socks', 'those with blonde hair', 'those with a

1976 1p piece in their pocket'. There are infinite variations.

To get everyone thoroughly roused, have an occasional request which will necessitate all players moving, e.g. 'all those wearing shoes', or 'all those with a nose', or 'all those with two ears'.

27 CHARACTER CHANGE

You will need a watch, two suitcases with all kinds of voluminous clothes and accessories: Boots, hats, handbags, school caps and scarves, furs, cloaks, dressing gowns, sporrans, even sheets or curtains.

Send the players to one end of the hall, and form into two lines. Each team member in turn must run to the far end of the room with his team's suitcase, unpack and don five items chosen for the funniest or most dramatic effect – or to resemble a character called out by the leader, such as Fagin, the Sheik, Julius Caesar – pose ten seconds for applause, then repack and bring back the case for the next in line.

Team award goes to the speediest line with a special prize for outstanding individual performance.

28 CHARLIE CHAPLIN RELAY

You will need a small ball or balloon, a bean bag, and a cane or stick per team.

Teams line up as for a normal relay race, but the distance to be covered must be short, say, 10 yards out and the same distance back. At the start of the race the bean bag, small ball and cane are placed on the ground in front of the first runner. On the starting signal he places the ball between his knees (where it must be retained throughout), the bean bag on his head, and the cane is retained in his hand. He then covers the required course, and hands everything over to the next to go. The cane must be twirled, Charlie Chaplin-fashion, while moving. If the ball or bean bag drops, it must be replaced immediately before moving on again.

29 CLIMBING THROUGH A NEWSPAPER

You will need plenty of old newspapers.

Relay teams, any number, line up at one end of a room. On the command 'Go' the Number 1 in each team rushes forward to the team's designated pile of papers, takes a page and tears a hole through which he passes. The snag – he must not break the outside edge of the paper, if he does he takes a new page and commences the process all over again. Having passed through the paper to the satisfaction of the referee (best to have one for each team) he rushes back to his team, touches hands with next competitor who repeats the sequence. The first team to successfully complete the exercise is the winner.

More hilarious, often ridiculously funny and much more difficult is to play the game in pairs. It's best to slim for a month before the event. An even more difficult variation is to make players play this game in pairs in a back to back position.

30 CONTAMINATION

Here is a hectic game. A contagious person is selected. Whoever he touches is immediately paralysed. He can only be brought back to life when a free person touches him. Mr. Contagious can win the game by rushing around touching every 'free' player.

31 CONTORTIONS

Players stand around in a room. The leader calls out parts of the body that must be put onto or next to an object. Each subsequent demand requires the players to get into more difficult positions. Anyone losing their balance is immediately counted out. The last survivor is the winner. Some ideas for commands:—

Elbow to wall, Nose on floor, Thumb on nose etc. Commands vary according to ability, age etc.

32 DETECTION

You will need a number of small objects in a cloth bag or pillowcase. Pencils and paper.

Players can touch (not feel) the items in the bag which is placed on a tray and passed around.

Contestants are allowed 15 seconds or so to touch the items. Players are then given time to write down the objects – as many as they can remember. The winner can be given a prize – perhaps one of the objects from the bag.

33 DETECTION SEARCH

You will need a number of miscellaneous small objects, see below, a list of each item and pencils and paper for each player.

The objects are secretly and discreetly given to each player as they arrive for the party. They are warned not to talk about the game. It's more fun if one or two players are exempt from this secret. Every player places the object on his person so that it can be observed, though camouflaged.

At a given signal, competitors search for the articles only using their eyes. On discovery they note down the object together with the name of the person and a description of the location of the article.

When a player completes the full number indicated by the host his list is checked privately while the game continues. A completed accurate list is the winning entry. To shorten the game, set a time limit. The player with the largest number of correct entries is declared the chief detective. A pair of toy handcuffs or a large badge could be awarded as a prize.

The M.C. should remember:
> To be certain of the location of the objects and name of player bearing each item.
> To announce at the beginning the number of items to be found.

Only eyes to be used to discover the objects, NOT hands.

The time limit.

The game becomes hilarious as each individual tries to achieve the maximum number of inspections, while everyone is anxious to be on the move hunting for themselves.

Some suggestions for camouflaged objects.
Piece of sellotape stuck on a man's collar.
Postage stamp on a woman's dress.
A wig: be careful whom you loan it to!
Cotton wound round string of beads.
Blob of silver paper on tie clip or brooch.
Hair pin in man's hair.
Black bootlace tied around a tie.
Cotton in hair or ear.
Extra button on a coat.
Brown shoelace in black shoes.
A small paper clip on a coat pocket flap.

34 DICTIONARY DEFINITIONS

You will require a dictionary, small sheets of paper for each player and a box.

Players sit in a semi-circle, one is chosen as the leader and handed the dictionary. A scorekeeper is appointed. The leader looks up a word in the dictionary and spells it out to the rest of the players. Each player writes down what he thinks the word means, the leader meanwhile writes down the dictionary definition. He puts this and all the players' definitions in a box and shuffles them. He then reads each paper out aloud. Each player votes for the one he thinks correct. Two points awarded to each player who has his definition chosen; and one point for choosing the correct definition. The dictionary is then passed to the next player who becomes the leader and the game continues.

35 DRESSING RACE

You will need a basket or bag containing hat, scarf, trousers, jacket, nightdress or dress for each team.

The players form into small teams of, say, five. A short distance from each team a basket or bag is placed containing the clothing, the items being roughly similar in each container. The first player in each team runs up to the basket, puts on all the clothes, picks up the basket and runs round the back of the team to replace the basket in its original position. He then takes off all the clothes, puts them in the basket, and runs back to his team to touch the second player, who does exactly the same thing all over again. The first team to finish is the winner.

36 DRAWING CLUMPS

You will need small sheets of paper and a supply of pencils. The leader has prepared a list of drawable objects or events, e.g. Monkey in a zoo, The Preacher in a pulpit, Coronation, a Cow being milked.

The leader sits apart from the guests who are divided into teams. A member from each team goes up to her and is given in confidence a different subject from her list. He returns to his group and has to draw the subject for the rest of his team to guess, without incorporating the words that will give the game away. Whoever guesses the subject goes up for the next on the list, until it is exhausted. The team exhausting the list first is the winner. There can be an additional prize for the funniest, simplest or best drawing.

37 DON'T CRACK

Any number of players sit on the floor cross-legged in a tightly knit circle. A leader is chosen who nudges the player on his left, who nudges the player on *his* left and so on round the circle. When the nudge reaches the leader, he tweaks the ear of the player on his left, who tweaks the ear of the player on *his* left and again so on round the circle. Next time, the leader pulls his neighbour's nose, or blows in his ear, or kisses his brow, or tickles him under the armpit or whispers something witty to him. Whatever the leader does, the others must do in quick succession. Speed is essential. Anyone who laughs or even smiles, is disqualified and leaves the circle. Whoever laughs last is the winner.

38 DUMB CRAMBO

About six people are sent out of the room. The rest decide on a word which those outside have to act, but they give them a word which rhymes with it. Those outside come in and act (dumb) all the words they can think of rhyming with the one they have been given until they act the chosen word (e.g. the word chosen is 'spark', and the players are told that it rhymes with 'lark'; they will therefore act 'mark', 'dark', etc., until they hit upon 'spark').

39 DUSTER HOCKEY

You will need two shinty sticks or walking-sticks with rounded tops, dusters or old socks made into a ball, and two chairs.

Two teams in line face each other, either sitting on chairs or standing behind a line as far away from each other as possible. Number the team members from opposite ends. Sticks and 'ball' are placed in the centre, and a chair at each end, which acts as a goal. The umpire calls a number, and two opponents rush out, pick up a stick, and attempt to score a goal by hitting the ball into their respective goals. When a goal is scored the equipment is replaced, and the umpire calls another number. Players must keep the sticks below shoulder-level.

40 EATING THE RAISINS

You will need two saucers and some raisins.

Two teams face each other at a distance of at least 5 feet apart. Both teams are numbered. Two saucers are placed in the centre of the teams containing a sprinkling of raisins. A number is called, and the player so numbered from each team rushes to the centre, and on their knees, with their hands behind their backs, they must eat the raisins. Points are awarded for the first to finish each time.

41 EDITORS NIGHTMARE

You will need a collection of mixed newspapers. Players are placed in groups around the room.

From a pile of mixed newspapers cut out different pieces – photographs, advertisements, columns of type of varying lengths. Keep the papers and distribute them to the different teams. Pile the cuttings in the middle of the floor, and let each team send one member to collect a piece which they have to fit into their newspaper, jigsaw fashion. If it does not belong, it is returned to the pile and another taken in its place. First team to complete its paper is winner.

42 EGG TRAIL

You will need an equal number of eggs and cake cases filled with cornflakes and a blindfold. Send a small number of the players out of the room.

A trail of eggs is then laid out. Players return individually, they are given a sight of the trail and then blindfolded. They are then told to walk the trail without stepping on the eggs. Just before they begin substitute cake cases filled with cornflakes for the eggs. Spectators encourage them suitably e.g. 'good', 'step higher', 'nearly'. The player is surprised when the blindfold is removed at the end of the walk.

43 ELASTIC BANDS

You will need an elastic band for each player.

Each player puts an elastic band over his face so that it comes just beneath the nose and ears. The idea of the game is to wriggle the face until the band comes underneath the chin. This can be played as a team game, with the band being passed down the team.

44 ELECTRIC SHOCK

You will need a chair, string, a cotton-reel, and a flower pot.

The players form into two teams of equal number. The leader stands one end and clasps hands with one member of each team. All the other members join hands. A chair separates other end of team. One side holds a string with a cotton-reel attached, resting on the chair; the other side holds a flower-pot poised over the cotton-reel. The leader starts the race by squeezing the hand of each end team member at the same time. The squeeze is passed along the line until it is received by the team member at the other end of the line. Now it is a race for the cat (flower-pot) to catch the mouse (cotton-reel) before the mouse can get away. The holders of the flower-pot and cotton-reel may only act when they receive a squeeze from their next door neighbour. After each attempt, the person holding the flower-pot or cotton-reel goes to the other end of the team and joins hands with the leader, so that each person has a turn of being 'cat' and 'mouse'. Points are awarded for the number of successful catches. A gong can be used instead of the flower-pot and cotton-reel.

45 FACE TO FACE

You will need strings of licorice.

Strings about 1–2 metres long are given to pairs, preferably boy and girl. Starting at opposite ends couples nibble and eat until they meet.

Have several strings crossing each other like the main strands of a spider's web for more amusement. Any breakages disqualify the couple from the game.

46 FEATHER FOOTBALL

You will need a feather (small to medium), two teams and a table.

The two teams gather on two sides of the table. The feather is 'launched' by the umpire who, being strictly impartial, seeks to launch it each time in centre of table. By blowing, the teams try to send the feather over the edge of the table on the opposition's side. Each time a team is successful they score a point. Before the game commences fix on a number to constitute as the winning total.

Half time, changing ends and any other variations can be improvised.

47 FIND THE ROUTE

You will need a small supply of local bus and rail timetables.

Sort out beforehand half-a-dozen difficult but not impossible journeys, including plenty of changing and plenty of possible alternatives. Divide the players into teams, give them a timetable each, and their instructions: e.g. 'The first team to find a way from Little End to Battersborne in less than two hours on a Saturday evening after seven o'clock.'

48 FIND YOUR PARTNER

There are two ways of playing this game.

(*a*) Write the names of missionaries on some slips of paper, and on others write the countries with which these missionaries are associated. Mix the papers and distribute among the players until none is left. Players who have the names of missionaries have to find their country, and *vice versa*. The person who has paired off most of his slips in the shortest time wins.

(*b*) Write the Christian names and surnames of missionaries on separate slips of paper, and play as (*a*).

This is a suitable game to play at a rally or party. Pioneer as well as present-day missionaries and nationals should be included.

49 FIND YOUR WATCH

You will need identical thick envelopes, and pencils.

Each participant puts his watch into an envelope. The M.C. shuffles the envelopes then numbers them. Players pick up the envelopes by a corner only – no feeling – and guess which is their possession by the tick. Frightfully difficult. Be careful, the packages need handling with care to avoid Insurance claims!

50 FLAPPING THE KIPPER

You will need two pieces of paper cut in the shape of a kipper, two boxes, and two rolls of newspaper.

The players form into teams and stand behind a line about 12 inches from the boxes. Each team member, with a roll of newspaper, flaps the kipper from behind the line into the box, and returns the kipper to the next member of the team in line.

51 GOODY-BAG TOUCH

You will need a strong bag of sweets, fruit, biscuits or cake.

Players stand in a circle apart from one odd man who stands in the circle holding the edibles. This man tosses the bag to anyone in the circle. The receiver catches the bag and runs round the outside of the circle, pursued by the thrower who tries to tag him before he can get back to the safety of his place in the circle.

If the thrower fails he goes into the centre and throws the bag to someone else. If he fails to tag the second time he is out. A signal is given to cease playing at a time decided by the leader. The last person catching the bag keeps the contents.

52 GRAB THE LOOT

You will need a pile of odds and ends.

Two teams line up at opposite ends of the playing

area. The articles are dumped in a pile in the centre of the area. When the game is started players rush and take back one item at a time to their base. They keep collecting until the pile is exhausted. Items are counted.

The team with most items is the winner.

53 GUESS WHO

You will need a white sheet.

A white sheet is hung across the room and a light is shone on to it. The players divide into two teams and members of one team take it in turns to walk across the room behind the sheet so that their shadows are thrown on to it. The opposing team sits in front guessing who it is going by. Obviously, the shadow players must do all they can to disguise their silhouettes. After each member of the first team has crossed the room at least twice, the teams swap round. At the end of the game, the team with the most correct guesses wins.

Variation: imitating well known characters and acting out some of their distinctive features.

54 GUIDE DOG

You will need a chair and a scarf for every pair of players.

Chairs are spaced around the room. The boy player is blindfolded and is guided round by his girl 'dog' while the music plays. When it stops the 'dog' has to guide her blind man to the nearest chair, sit him down, and then sit on his knee. Pairs without a chair are out.

55 HANDLEBAR WHISKERS

You will need some burnt corks, paper towels and flannels.

The male partner sits on a chair; his female assistant stands behind the chair. On the command 'Go' the female attempts to crayon, with the burnt cork, 'whiskers' down to the chin on her man.

The most artistic set of whiskers is declared the winning entry.

56 HANDS, FEET, AND HEAD

You will need paper and pencils for all players.

After all the players have been provided with paper and pencils they are requested to make five dots on any part of the paper they like — scattered about, close together, or even in a straight line. The papers are then collected shuffled and redealt, and the leader of the game explains that the dots represent the exact position of a man's hands, his feet, and his head. Each player is expected to draw the figure of a man with his hands, feet, and head in the position represented by the dots upon the paper before them.

57 HAPPY FAMILIES

You will need a number of groups of three cards, each group for a different family, e.g. Father Blot, Mother Blot, and Baby Blot, choosing silly names.

Groups of three chairs are placed round the room, one group less than the number of families. The cards are jumbled up and placed on four chairs in corners of the room. Players seat themselves in threes, and on the word 'Go' rush to the corner chairs to pick up a card, and then try to find the other members of their 'family'. As soon as they do so they rush to get a group of chairs (the original threes must not be disturbed). The 'family' that is left standing is eliminated, their cards are handed in, and three chairs removed. Players return their cards to one of the corner chairs, and march round until a whistle blows, when the whole performance is repeated. The 'family' left at the end is of course the winner.

58 HERE WE GO GATHERING NUTS

You will need 2 chairs, 2 plastic bowls, 2 hand mirrors, 2 spoons and a bag of peanuts.

This is a game for 2 teams who assemble at one end of the room. They approach the chairs in pairs.

One player in each pair sits in a chair, with a tablespoon in one hand and an empty plastic bowl on his head. (He is allowed to steady the bowl with his free hand.) His partner stands in front of him with a mirror in one hand and a bowl of peanuts in the other. The first player spoons the nuts from his partner's bowl to the bowl on his own head, guiding himself by looking into the mirror.

The pair who get the most nuts into their bowl win points for their side.

59 HISSING AND CLAPPING

Half the company stand behind chairs, each of which bears the name of a country or a town. The other half go out, and each is handed the name of a missionary, past or present. Each returns singly to the room and sits down on the chair he considers is associated with the missionary whose name is on the slip. If he sits down on the correct chair, everyone claps; if not, all hiss, and he tries again until successful. (This is an excellent way of helping young people to associate missionaries with their countries or stations. Suitable for revision, or to impress the spread of the Church overseas.)

60 HOWSAT! HOWSAT!

You will need a paper with the following diagram, one to be given to each player.

Each player attempts to get a vertical or horizontal line of signatures. The first to do so shouts 'Howsat'. If his paper has a line of signatures he is declared the winner. A good mixing and 'getting to know you' game.

	1	2	3	4	5	6
H						
O						
W						
S						
A						
T						

61 HOW OFTEN DO YOU?

One player is sent out of the room, and a certain action is chosen, e.g. threading a needle; cooking dinner; bathing a baby; trimming a moustache. The person is then called into the room and is asked five or six questions by the leader: e.g. 'How often do you do it?' 'What time of day do you do it?' 'What does your wife say when you do it?' 'What do the police say when you do it?' 'Where do you do it?' When the person has answered the questions he is told what the action was.

62 HUMAN HAPPY FAMILIES

You will need one movable chair per player.

This game is suitable for twenty to fifty players. The leader chooses a different character, real or imaginary, living or dead, for each player to represent. He whispers his choice in the ear of each player in turn. No player is allowed to tell anyone else the name of the character chosen for him. In selecting characters for players it is best to make them extremely appropriate or extremely inappropriate if this can be managed. The leader then reads to all the players a complete list of the characters present. He should do this twice at slow speed, but players should not be permitted to take notes.

The players are then divided into groups of five or six (the exact number does not matter), and they sit down on their chairs in those groups. Play begins when one group asks another group for a character whose name they have heard read out in the list. For example, they may ask for Little Miss Muffett. If she is in the group asked, she leaves that group and goes to join the group who have asked for her, taking her chair with her. The group who have made this correct guess then have another turn. If any guess by a group proves incorrect, it is the group who were asked for, and were wrongly thought to have, the character who have the next turn.

When a group's turn comes to do the asking, their first guess must be of the whereabouts of a character whose identity has not been revealed previously in the game. If they are successful, they may then ask the first group for Little Miss Muffett. Members of a group can co-operate with each other before asking for a character, but only one person in the group does the asking. The same person need not always be the spokesman. Players should not tell their identity, even to others in their own group. If a group is thinking of asking for a character who is one of their number already, it is usually possible for the player concerned to advise against this without actually revealing his identity.

During play some groups disappear altogether and others grow larger and smaller alternately. The final outcome of the game is that all players are gathered into one group. After about half the characters have been identified, the leader should refresh the memories of the players by reading out a list of those characters who are still unidentified.

63 HUMAN SPELLING

You will need fifty-two players and two sets of letters of the alphabet, large enough to be seen in a reasonably large hall.

Every letter of the alphabet should be included in the list of words.

Divide players into two teams, giving each team a set of letters. Each individual player is given a card and the teams are lined up opposite one another.

The leader shouts out a word from the list and the players holding the appropriate letters step one pace forward and arrange themselves in the order of the word from right to left.

The first team to spell its word properly with the letters held up above their heads scores a point.

The chosen words should not contain repeated letters.

64 I'M ...... WHO ARE YOU?

You will need prepared question papers and plenty of slips of paper with 10 chosen objects on them.

Players mill around the room talking to others. They must always begin the conversation with the formula as under. They can then ask for an object which the leader has announced at the commencement. When in private conversation the person who is designated by the object is found (e.g. a 'waste paper basket') without fuss and with maximum secrecy, a slip of paper is given by 'waste paper basket' bearing the next 'thing' on the list. The person who through questioning collects 10 object slips is the winner. Each designated person must have suffi-

cient slips of paper to give one to each player if
necessary.

I'm ....(give your own name)

What is your name?

My wife or friend's name is ....

Are you a ....?

Suggestions for Designations.

Waste paper bin

Big Ben

A squashed tomato

Pink elephant

A Bent Bentley

A wee sweet (they receive a Rowntrees gum)

Blue Battleship

A Pork Pie

A Kangaroo

65 INTRODUCTIONS

You will need 10 matchsticks for each guest

As the guests arrive, the host gives each of them 10
matchsticks. A guest then takes a number of his
matchsticks in one hand and holds out his clenched
fist to any other guest, demanding, 'odd or even?'
The other guest gives his answer and if he has guessed correctly, the man holding the matchsticks
hands over one of them to his opponent. The opponent then goes through the same routine with some
of his own matches. If the original questioner guesses incorrectly he hands over another match, but if
his guess is correct he now collects a match from his
opponent.

When the time is up, the player with the greatest
number of matchsticks is the winner.

66 KEEP GOSSIPING

A getting to know you game. Two concentric circles
are formed, the men facing outwards and the
women facing inwards; music is played and the
circle dance round. When the music stops everyone
must talk to the person immediately opposite them

for one minute on a topic to be announced by the host. The pairs must exchange views, e.g. 'Noses I have pinched', 'Value Added Tax' or 'My most embarrassing moment'. When the one minute has passed the music strikes up again and the circles dance round once more. Once all the topics (6 or 8 would be sufficient) have been exhausted and everyone appears to have been exposed to the views of everyone else, the leader announces the Moment of Truth. In fact, the 'moment' lasts a minute, during the course of which the players rush about the room trying to catch hold of the individual with whom they feel most in sympathy.

This can be followed by a game in which the pairs participate.

67 JOURNALISTS

You will need paper and pencils, an equal number of fellows and girls and also a room to which the men can be sent.

Without being told the aim of the game, men and women are placed in pairs and they are asked to converse with their partner for one minute. The men are then led to the other room, with their partners out of sight.

They are then told they are journalists and are asked to write down a description of their partner, e.g. what she looked like, what she was wearing, etc.

The M.C. returns to the main hall and informs the whole party what the men are doing.

After about five minutes, the men are recalled and are asked to read their descriptions, which are usually so hopelessly inaccurate that there is great mirth!

68 JUMBLED NAMES

You will need a number of cards with jumbled names of places and people, pencils and paper.

The cards are placed round the room and the players provided with paper and pencils. The cards should be printed clearly and numbered, e.g. LEN-GRLEF – GRENFELL; IMAJACA – JAMAICA; RYN-MAT – MARTYN, etc. (The places can be found afterwards on a map, particularly when the game is used as an introduction for study of a country.)

69 KIM'S GAME

You will need paper and pencil for each player, and the objects mentioned below.

There are many variations of this game:

(1) Players sit in a circle, and a tray containing twenty or more objects is passed round, each player noting the contents. The tray is then withdrawn and paper and pencils distributed, and the objects on the tray are listed from memory.

(2) A number of bottles or jars filled with scented objects are passed round the circle of players, who list the contents as they smell them. (Contents can vary from a particular perfume to a bad herring.)

(3) A number of objects are placed in opaque bags and passed round the circle for identification. Alternatively this can be done in the dark, in which case the players memorize the objects and list them at the end. (Have some articles which are similar in shape, such as a button and a drawing-pin.)

70 KNIGHTS AND LADIES

You will need a small book for each player.

The players form two circles, girls on the inside, boys on the outside, each balancing a small book on their heads. When the music starts they all parade around, girls one way, boys the other. When the music stops the boys and girls turn to face each other; the boys bow, and the girls curtsey. If a book is dropped, that pair is eliminated. The last pair left in are the winners.

71 LETTER-CHANGING

The players sit in a circle and somebody chooses a word, preferably a three-lettered one, but four letters is satisfactory with advanced players. The next player makes a different word by changing one letter of the original word. The third player takes the second word and deals with it in the same way; thus the changes proceed as each fresh player's turn is reached. A word like 'fun' might become fin, tin, tie, pie, pit, sit, sat, mat, rat, etc. A word once given must not be repeated. If a player cannot make a completely new word, he drops out of the game, and an entirely fresh word is chosen by the next player. The one who is left in to the last is the winner.

72   LIB DAYS!

You will need large pile of buttons, as many pieces of cloth as there are players, a large reel of cotton, needles, pieces of wood, one for each lady, a packet of tacks, and a hammer for each lady.

At a given signal, all the men dive into a pile of buttons, each taking a handful, threading his needle, and endeavouring to sew on as many buttons as possible in a given time – say ten minutes. When time is 'up', the referee (who must be appointed before the commencement of the game) collects the pieces of cloth and counts the number of buttons on each. The man who has sewn on the largest number is the male winner.

Each lady is now given a piece of wood about 450 mm × 150 mm, and about 45 mm thick; four or five dozen tacks; and a hammer. A certain time is then given in which they must hammer as many tacks as possible into the boards before them. At the expiration of the time a count is made. The largest number of nails driven into the wood is the target for the ladies' champion.

Suitable funny prizes can be awarded.

73   LINE DRAWINGS

You will need pencils and several sheets of paper for each group.

The leader describes how to draw an object without

telling the players what it is. E.g. 'Draw a horizontal line 72 mm long, 2 short vertical lines at each end underneath and joining the horizontal.' This is a table. As they draw each stage, the players have to guess what it is they are drawing, and the first to guess correctly stands up and gives instructions for drawing the next object.

74 MILKO!

You will need 2 chairs, rubber gloves, 2 aprons, water and 2 buckets.
Divide players into 2 teams.

Make small holes in each finger, oт rubber gloves, fill with water, and hang from each chair. Players are given a time limit to milk the 'cow' into the bucket, on a whistle blast the next player rushes forward, dons the apron and continues the process. The team who first milks the 'cow' dry are winners.

Caution, have additional rubber gloves and some absorbent floor covering in case of accidents.

75 MIMING GAME

About six people are sent out of the room. Those left inside decide what they will ask the people outside to act (one at a time), e.g. bathing a baby, making a cake, starting up a car after backing out of the garage. The first person comes in and is told what to act. The second comes in and watches, and then copies what he has seen to the third to come in. This continues until all outside have come in. The last one has to guess what the previous one was doing. If possible, the first person should repeat his act for the benefit of the guesser, and to the amusement of the rest.

76 MOVE ROUND AND PILE UP

You will need a strong chair for each player.

Chairs are arranged as in 'Changing Places', but no one is eliminated, neither can anyone win.

The object of this game is purely good entertainment. When the M.C. calls, participants must move quickly. He says, for example, 'All the girls with black shoes move two places to the left.' They all have to move and if the chair two places to the left is occupied, they simply sit on the player who is already there.

It can be seen that as the game proceeds, many players get stacked on to one chair, much to the delight and agony of participants.

77 MUSICAL CLOTHES

You will need a bag of assorted clothes – hats, coats, trousers, skirts, baby's bibs, gloves, etc., allowing four or five garments for each player.

Players are seated in a circle, the music starts and the bag is passed round clockwise. The person holding it when the music stops must take out one garment and put it on. The bag continues on its journey with a garment being extracted each time the music stops. When the bag is empty the reverse process starts, and players replace one of the garments they have previously taken out each time the music stops. The first person to return all his extra garments is the winner.

78 MUSICAL COUPLES

You will need a chair for every two players, minus one.

The chairs should be placed down the centre of the room with each one facing in the opposite direction from its neighbour. While the music is playing the contestants walk round the line of chairs in pairs. When the music stops each pair runs for a chair; the boy sits on the chair, with the girl on his knee. The pair without a chair are out. A further chair is removed, and the game continues until one pair is left. For a change, the boys can sit on the girls' knees.

79 MY COMPANION SNORES!

Good for adults and young newly marrieds. Players sitting in a circle, husbands and wives take it in turn to be blindfolded. The unblindfolded partners make snoring sounds while the blindfolded mates move around trying to detect their partners and sit on their lap. Made more complicated if those sitting change places while the game is in progress.

80 NEXT DOOR NEIGHBOUR

This is an ideal game where everybody is well known. One person is sent out of the room, and the rest are informed that 'Mr. X' is the person on their left. The exile is recalled, and told that the group has nominated a 'Mr. X', and that he can be identified by the asking and answering of questions. The resulting confusion can only be imagined. Honours graduates sometimes discover who 'Mr. X' really is!

81 NOSEY

You will need an old sheet with a hole just big enough for a nose.

Couples are chosen from among the players. Each man runs his finger over the bridge of the nose of his partner – so he knows just what her nose looks like! The girls are placed behind the sheet. One by one they put their nose through the hole. The boys on the other side are sent out of the room; appearing one by one, they have to make up their minds which is their partner. If they think it is their 'girl' they have to rush forward and kiss the nose. They only have one chance. If mistaken they are eliminated. A small prize can be given to successful pairs.

82 NOTICES

You will need notices to hang round the wall, and pencils and paper for each player.

The players have to guess what public notices are indicated from the initials only of each word in the notice, e.g. 'Please Keep Off The Grass' (putting on the card only P K O T G); 'No exit'; 'Halt Major Road Ahead'; 'Do Not Alight From Moving Train'; 'No Smoking', etc. Each notice should be printed on a separate card and hung round the walls.

83 OFF TO WORK

You will need a hat and a newspaper for every girl player.

The boys stand at one end of the room with jackets over their arms, shirts and ties unfastened. The girls, at the opposite end of the room, have a hat and a folded newspaper at their feet. On the word 'Go', the girls rush to their partners, fasten up shirts, tie ties and help them on with their jackets. Each girl runs back for the hat, brings it to her partner and puts it on his head; then she rushes back for the newspaper to hand to him. Together they run for the door, where she kisses him goodbye and pushes him out of the door. The first pair to finish wins.

84 ONE MINUTE, PLEASE

You will need some slips of paper and a hat.

Sitting in a circle, the players are invited to take a slip of paper out of the hat. Some will draw blanks; others will have a subject for a one-minute speech. Players speak on their subject in turn, and their speeches are judged by the volume of applause from the audience. (Suggested topics: 'Dog collars'; 'Ladies' Contemporary Hats'; 'The Glories of Wales'; 'Haggis of Scotland'; 'The Most Interesting Character I have ever met', etc.)

85 PAPER CHASE

You will need one newspaper to each team of 5 or 6 people.

Huddled in close circles, the team is given a mixed up newspaper. On the command 'Go' contestants reassemble the paper in the correct order. Make sure the papers are the same size. First team to complete are the winners.

86 PICTURES AND PUZZLES

You will need to collect pictures from old magazines cut out and pasted on cardboard.

The pieces are distributed amongst the players who are divided into 2 or more teams; the teams try to complete a picture. Pieces can be swopped on a one for one exchange rate. The team to complete a picture first wins the game.

Can be played with two or any number of players.

87 PORK AND BEANS

The players are divided into pairs, and on the word 'Go' one of each pair starts asking the other questions. The partner must keep an absolutely straight face, and answer to every question 'Pork and beans'. If he smiles or laughs at all he is out of the game. The couple who can keep up the questioning and answering the longest are the winners.

88 POST

You will need a blindfold.

One player, who must be blindfolded, acts as the postman. Another is chosen for postmaster. The rest of the players seat themselves round the room.

The postmaster then gives to each the name of a town. The blind postman is now placed in the middle of the room, and the postmaster takes the position where he can overlook the players. When all are ready he calls out 'A letter has been sent from (naming a town represented by one of the players) to (here he gives the name of another town).' The two players representing the towns mentioned must immediately change places, the object of the postman being to either capture them or sit down in one of the unoccupied chairs before the player has time to reach it. The player who is caught, or whose chair the postman has taken, becomes postman in his stead.

89 POST BOX

You will need a number of boxes with place names written on them. For each player a set of cards with all the place names written one to a card.

Boxes are hidden around the garden or hall. On command 'Go' players have to post letters in the corresponding box. The player making the quickest delivery round is the winner.

Variation: Instead of boxes, people can be used. This 'checks' the letters and avoids any malpractice.

90 PROVERBS

You will need proverbs written on cards, and paper and pencils for the players.

On cards write out parts of proverbs; for instance, on one card write 'Too many', and on another card 'cooks spoil', and on a third, 'the broth', etc. Hide two cards in different places from each set of proverbs, and distribute the remaining cards among the players. Each player will have to work out from his card what the whole proverb is, and then find it. The first player to produce a whole proverb is the winner.

91 QUICK QUESTIONS

Players stand in a circle with one in the centre who throws some soft object at any player he chooses, at the same time calling out a question of a missionary character. If the player does not reply before the questioner counts ten, he takes his place in the centre and asks the next question. (This game is suitable for revision of a story or series of lessons, as well as for testing general knowledge.)

92 QUICK THINK

You will need paper and pencils for each player.

A number of categories are chosen, usually five or six, such as Towns, Cities, Animals, Names, Families, Trees or Flowers. A letter in the alphabet is then taken at random, and players have two minutes or longer to write down as many words in each category as they can, which begin with that letter.

93 SAUSAGES AND MASH

Players sit in a tight circle around a victim. They fire questions at him, his only reply being 'Sausages and mash'. Any player smiling is counted out. The last remaining player is the winner.

The funnier the questions, the quicker the game runs to a conclusion.

Some sample questions:
    'What is Joan's hair like?'
    'What is the shape of your tongue?'
    'What are you sitting on?'

94 SCOOP

You will need several sheets of paper and a pencil for each player.

Players are divided into two teams, those with artistic talent being allocated evenly, and all are given several sheets of paper and pencils. Each team is given an account of an event which has recently appeared in the news, and they must illustrate this. The best arrangement is to give each member of the team one part of the news item, so that there are four or five single drawings showing different stages of the incident. The teams are allowed ten minutes in which to finish their drawings, after which they exchange drawings, and try to guess the news story from the pictures. The leader should write out the story with a fair amount of detail, so that the teams have plenty of scope for their drawings. If, for instance, it is the story of a train crash, he should give information as to the time, the place, how the accident happened, what happened afterwards, and what other people were doing at the time.

95 SIGNATURES

You will need duplicated question papers and pencils for all players.

A 'make friends' game. A good party starter. Each person receives the questions as they arrive and moves around the room asking others questions and gaining signatures from those for whom the statements are true. When time is called the person with the largest number of signatures is declared the winner.

A sample questionnaire. Make up your own with local interests in mind.

Can ski (snow) ....

Commutes to town each day ....

Is wearing three rings ....

Takes size 5 in shoes ....

Plays an instrument ....

Has sung a solo ....

Is happy on rising in the morning ....

Finds it difficult to get up in the morning ....

Prefers own company ....

Makes own clothes ....

Cooks well ....

You know his or her peculiarities ....

Doesn't like strawberries ....

Talks a lot ....

Is overweight ....

Dislikes diets (slimming) ....

Has no need to slim ....

Is about 40 years but looks in early 30's ....

Has flown in aeroplane this year ....

Has a good bedside manner ....

Has eaten this year ....

'Tail of a kine that hangs behind' ....

Can do Hokey Kokey ....

Is left-handed ....

Only reads non-fiction books ....
Has an unfulfilled ambition ....

96 SMELLS GALORE

You will need small bags of herbs, flowers or veget-
ables which have a distinct aroma.

Small bags, each numbered and containing the
individual items for smelling. Give players a paper
with a copy of all the items. The players have to
identify the contents and place the number of the
bag by the item on the list. First to complete total list
is the winner.

Variations: Instead of plants, use cheeses – Stilton,
Cheshire, Danish Blue etc.
    Perfumes or other liquids are an alternative.

97 SPILL THE BEANS

You will need five beans (or dried peas or matches)
for each player.

Each player is given five beans (or dried peas or
matches) and told that the object of the game is to
talk to someone and try to make him say 'Yes' or
'No' by asking questions, or by any other means
they can think of. If successful, they have to hand
over a bean to the unfortunate one who has said
'Yes' or 'No', and move on to someone else. The first
person to get rid of all his beans is the winner.

98 STORY-TELLING

You will need six objects.

The objects are placed on a tray, and four or so
persons are selected. They are given a few moments
to look at the objects, and then asked to tell a story in
two minutes which will bring in all the objects on the
tray. The players come in one by one, so that each
has equal notice of the objects involved. The winner
is estimated by the volume of applause.

99 SUSPECT

The leader is the detective; he tells a simple story which has brought him in his search to the location of the party. As the crime is one of theft he wants to find the person in the room who has the most objects in his pocket or handbag. It is extraordinary what people carry in these receptacles! The player found to have the most objects is presented with a prize (a pair of toy handcuffs or some other booby prize).

100 SWOPPING

The players sit in a large circle, and one person stands in the middle to announce which players are to change places. As they change, he tries to get a seat, and the person left standing takes his place in the middle. The important thing is to get the game moving quickly, and to ask players to make original announcements when their turn comes for being in the middle. For instance, they could ask everyone who has been abroad to change places; or those who did not shave before noon; or people who have had a birthday this month – there are hundreds of variations.

101 TELEGRAMS

You will need a 'Telegram' form as under for each player and a pencil.

A	C	B	T	D
G	F	N	Y	S
D	B	B	N	O
C	T	L	S	O
W	T	V	T	A

Players have to make up telegrams to fit the letters. For instance the bottom line could read – 'Watch Tele-Vision Tonight Appearing'. A time limit is set, the person with the greatest number of filled in lines is the winner.

102 THAWING ICE

You will need a number of ice cubes. Two or more teams of 6 or more members in each team.

A small cube of ice, each of an identical size is given to each team. Passing the cube from player to player, the team which melts the ice, eliminating it first is the winner.

103 THE MANDARINS

The players all draw their chairs into a circle, and one of them commences the game by saying 'My ship has come home from China.' Her next-door neighbour says 'Really! and what has it brought?' The first player replies 'A fan'; and begins to fan herself with her right hand, all the other players immediately copying her. The second player then turns to the next with the same remark. When asked what her ship has brought, she says 'Two fans' and commences to fan herself with both hands. On hearing that a ship has brought home three fans, the players all nod their heads, keeping their hands on the move the whole time. And so on, until by the time seven has been reached, hands, heads, arms, legs, feet, eyes and mouth are all moving. The fun lies in watching the movements of the other players who in their turn are amused over the absurdity of your own movements.

104 THINK OF A WORD

Players sit in a circle, the leader calls on someone to think of a word and call it out loudly. The player on the right of the caller must say a word associated with the first. The cycle of associated words continues with each player on the right calling a word. Anyone pausing is out.

Example: Field grass, sheep wool, lambs chops, teeth comb, etc.

(105) THREE-LEGGED MUSICAL CHAIRS

You will need music, chairs for a third of the players, scarves or cords to join three people at the ankles.

Players in three, the centre person sits two others on his knee. When the music commences trios walk around outside the chairs which have been set in the largest circle possible. When music stops trios sit down on chairs. One chair is removed each time the music starts. The last trio to be seated each time is eliminated. The winners are the last seated when only one chair remains.

106 TITLE MIMING

You will need a list of well known book titles, film titles or songs, hymns or carols, or radio and television programmes.

Each player chooses a title from the list or is given one by the leader; he takes his turn in miming it for the rest of the group to guess.

He can mime either the whole title or divide his performance into 'scenes' each representing a word or syllable.

The player getting the maximum number of correct answers is the winner.

107 TRUSSING

You will need handkerchiefs or suitable material for binding hands together, and two broomsticks.

Can be played as a competitive team game.

2 boys seated on the floor. Each player's hands are bound together palm to palm; feet are also tied together at the ankles. Legs are drawn up under chins, heels resting on the floor. Arms pass over the knees, hands joined. The broomstick is passed over the arms and under the knees.

This resembles a skewer trussing a chicken.

Competitors are placed toe to toe opposite each other.

The object is to turn the opponent on his back or

side by use of his toes.
Points are scored for the winning team.

108 TUNNEL RELAY

You will need a tunnel made of canvas or stout cloth about 600 cms long and 90 cms in diameter.

Two teams compete, entering the tunnel from opposite ends. Only two players are allowed in the tunnel at any time. The inevitable passing point can give plenty of spectator value.

The first team with each member clear of the tunnel is the winner.

109 TUBE STATIONS

You will need prepared papers and pencils for each participant. For those unfamiliar with the London Underground system maps and charts are available from London Transport.

Players have to find the appropriate answers to the 24 clues in a given time. Maximum correct answers herald the winner.

1. Egg shaped
2. Dark monks
3. Home of Moriarty's enemy
4. Continental retreat
5. Top people's open space
6. What a holy man uses for bowling
7. Do rabbits live here?
8. Where you lose your head
9. Coloured river crossing
10. The disconsolate widow
11. Priest's field
13. Sounds as if a football team captured the street
14. Won on the playing fields of Eton
15. Canine cries
16. John O'Gaunt's portal
17. Shakespeare country
18. Royal Road
19. Leave your money here
20. 1,760 yards gone
21. Rough seas do this to some people
22. This dyke needs supporting

12. Place for spreading the good news

23. Burial place for sappers
24. No gate across this lane.

ANSWERS

1. Oval
2. Blackfriars
3. Baker Street
4. Swiss Cottage
5. Park Royal
6. Parsons Green
7. Warren Street
8. Tower Hill
9. Redbridge
10. Victoria
11. Canons Park
12. Gospel Oak
13. Tottenham Court Road
14. Waterloo
15. Barking
16. Lancaster Gate
17. Stratford
18. Queensway
19. Bank
20. Mile End
21. Turnham Green
22. Shoreditch
23. Gunnersbury
24. Turnpike Lane

110 TWOS AND THREES

You will need sufficient chairs for players.

The chairs are arranged round the room in groups of three. If possible the centre chair in each group should be occupied by a boy, who should have a girl on either side of him. One centre player should have only one partner, the seat on the other side of him being vacant. When the music begins this centre player and his one partner go to another group and grab another player from either of the side chairs. The centre player who has thus been deprived of a partner then goes and grabs another partner from somewhere else. Play proceeds until the music stops. The last centre player who has successfully grabbed a partner before the music stops is out of the game with both his partners. They remove their chairs from the arena, and the music begins again. The winners are the last three players to survive.

111 VIOLENT MUSICAL CHAIRS

You will need one chair to every other player.

The chairs are arranged in a circle facing outwards. The players are divided into two equal groups. If there are an equal number of boys and girls, then the boys form one group and the girls the other. One group stands inside the circle of chairs, each player in that group grasping a firm hold of one chair in the circle. The players inside the circle remain in this same position throughout the first round of the game, and their object is to see that the chairs are not moved during play. Each of the other players sits on one of the chairs which is to be his chair for the whole of the round. Each player takes note of the person standing behind his chair. The music starts, and all the players who have been sitting get up and walk round the outside of the circle of chairs in the same direction. When the music stops the players run back to their own chairs and sit down. The last one to sit down is out, but remains seated on his chair for the rest of the round. Play goes on until the final is decided between the last two players. For the next round the players inside the circle of chairs change places with those outside, and it is their turn to be exhausted. To hasten play the leader can decree that two players or more will be out each time the music stops.

112 VISITOR

The players are divided into groups of six. Each group sends its first player into the next group. The leader announces that the visitor has to name as many flowers as possible beginning with a certain letter; or name as many makes of car as possible; or girls' names beginning with a certain letter; or something similar. The visitor has to do this as best he can while the group, by talking and laughing, are trying to prevent him. After 'Time' has been called, the players return to their own groups with their scores, and the second two players go visiting.

Everyone in the team is given a turn, and group scores are added up to find the winner. (A good mixing game.)

113 WASHING DAY

You will need four lengths of rope or thick string, an assortment of clothes, and some pegs.

The players form into four teams of even numbers. Four washing lines are held across the hall. Each team lines up in front of one of the lines, and the first players are each given a pile of assorted clothes and some pegs, one peg more than there are garments. On the word 'Go' the first player rushes to the line to peg out the clothes, using all the pegs and clothes. He returns to his team, and the second player rushes to take down the washing, and so on through the team. The teams should be gone through twice so that everyone has a chance to hang up and take down the washing. The first team to finish is the winner.

Variation: Use human posts who wiggle, heighten or lower the line. This could be called 'Windy washing day'.

114 WEIGH IN

You will need bathroom scales, pencil and paper for judges.

Players are divided into two teams. Each person is taken into another room and weighed and weight recorded. The judge adds up the combined weight of each team.

The object of game is for each team to guess the weight of every member of the opposing team, and then guess the total weight of the team. Players can lift, prod, measure and converse with members of the opposite team.

The winning team is the one which gets closest to the combined weight of the opposite team.

115 EMERGENCY ACTION

You will need to prepare a Situation Report, pencils, designation cards and score cards (see note, below).

Aim: A serious game, designed to help people consider some of the needs of underprivileged countries. It can be adapted for a variety of needs and subjects.

It can be played by any number of participants. It needs careful preparation. Excellent as a mixing game at the commencement of a session or evening devoted to more serious issues of global involvement.

Procedure:
1. Read through the situational reports and choose your project.
2. On your answer paper state number of project clearly.
3. On the command 'Commence – Exchange' each player, who will have received 30 designation cards, can proceed to exchange them with other players in order to get maximum points.
4. During the exchange period the aim is to get as many of the designation cards that you require to build a development programme. The idea is to select the order of priority; the five most important items required, in your estimation, to meet the need of the situation. The judges have an approved order.
5. The game is won by the person or persons with the highest number of marks.
6. The exchange period will be brought to a conclusion by the caller announcing 'the bank is open'.
7. Participants can then trade only with the bank on a two for one basis. You give two into the bank and you receive one. You can exchange as many pairs as you wish. After about a ten minute period the bank is closed.

Scoring: Each individual works out his score as the judges outline the five items in order of priority required to meet the particular need of the project.

Example score card:

Example Situational reports

Note: Organisers can make up their own situational reports. These two are typical situations facing the Christian Church to-day.

1. Prolonged drought has made the hills and mountains of Ethiopia, particularly in the Wollo and Tegris province barren of crops and cattle. Hundreds of people have been trying to trek down the hills to the roadsides with their families in search of water, food and medical supplies. Thousands of bodies can be found on the main road, while thousands upon thousands of people are suffering from typhus, typhoid, malaria, beri-beri and malnutrition. The large pots which women carry are empty, the people appear bewildered and unbelieving, babies wail, the breasts of mothers being dried up and milkless. Men stand around looking aimless; they don't appear to have strength to engage in conversation or work. Most simply stand sit or squat and stare. Children look forlorn, thousands being orphans. There seems to be organized chaos, apparently few organisations are as yet alerted to the tremendous need of this situation.

What do you consider to be the priorities in a list for help?

2. As we move up river in the jungle of Irian Jaya in New Guinea, which is a part of the great galaxy of

islands in a great archipelago in which 128 million people live known to us as Indonesia, we realize there are many needs. Christianity came to this land in 1861 but it was not until 1936 that any real attempt was made to reach the isolated warring cannibal tribes in the mountains beyond the swamps. After the Second World War tribes became of great interest to the missionary societies. A church fellowship has been formed on this river and as we alight from our wooden boat we are met by two missionaries and their children and a group of happy faced tribespeople. Missionaries have been working here just over three years and the church now numbers just over 60. They have a missionary concern for other tribes and set sail in their log boats quite frequently on evangelistic tours. The missionary by training is a bible teacher, his wife a secretary. Illness and various diseases are a constant plague in this community and it is not infrequent that casualties from hunting are brought in from the jungle. The task of communicating to the wider area is a very real problem, for apart from mouth to mouth communication and the occasional evangelistic visits, no other programme can be undertaken at present.

How would you tackle these areas? What order or priority do you consider is required to build the church and to make it an evangelistic agency to its own people?

Designation cards
PERSONNEL AND EQUIPMENT AVAILABLE FOR YOUR PROJECT

Water supply	Doctor	Hospital
Electricity	Agricultural	Farm credit for
Tractor	adviser	seeds etc.
Drugs and pills	New Clothes	Blankets
Portable buildings	Spades and hand	Beds
Teacher	gardening tools	School

Occupational therapist	Bibles	Church building
Radios	Health worker	Animals, cows and goats
Evangelist	Builder	Policemen
Basic food	Mechanics	Nurse
Church planter	Organist	Secretary
Printer	Bible translator	Tools
Layout artist	Bible teacher	
	Business manager	

SECTION 9
PROGRAMME
FILLERS

It is often useful to have a few items for a few players, if only to give the whole group a breather. These suggestions all have spectator value.

1 APPLE BOBBING

You will need apples, onions, blindfolds, and wash bath or child's paddling pool.

Contestants are blindfolded and kneel, hands behind back, and at command 'Go' try to remove an apple from the tub filled with water. After they have been blindfolded, apples have been removed and onions substituted. Encouraged by spectators, players often splash around for a considerable time before they discover the hoax.

2 AGILITY

You will need matchboxes and chairs.

The boys will want to try this rather amusing test of agility. Place a matchbox on end behind the right-hand rear leg of a wooden chair. The object is to pick this up in one's teeth while remaining on the chair. If any part of the body touches the ground, the attempt has failed. It is possible, but very difficult.

③ BODY CHARADE

The group are divided into two 'A' and 'B', or appropriately named teams. Four persons from each group are selected to act, the rest of the team guess the words which they are spelling out by forming the letters in a 'body letter' of the alphabet (e.g. Two actors – back to back, arms outstretched form 'T'). No fingers may be used to form individual letters. Each group complete a word or phrase given by the M.C. and guessed by their team before asking the M.C. to whisper the next sentence.

Sample of phrase which could be used:

Two for tea.	Blow your nose.
How are you.	Nice day.
Keep quiet.	No Entry.
What's the time.	Goodnight.

4 BLINDFOLD DRESSING

You will need, 2 or 3 pairs of gardening gloves, 2 or 3 pairs of tights.

Selected players are given a pair of gardening gloves and then blindfolded. They have to remove shoes and then put on a pair of tights or panty hose. First to get both legs clad to the knees is the winner.

5 CLOSE SHAVE

You will need blindfolds, soap, spatulas, towels.

2 or more boys sit on chairs with a blindfolded female partner standing behind each chair.

Each girl has to cream and shave the face of her partner. The best shave in a given time is declared the winner. Warning – suitable towel around the shoulders of the boy, and use wooden spatula.

6 HEAD THROUGH POSTCARD

You will need a pair of scissors and a postcard for each player.

The competition is for the first player to put his head through the card.

After some time has elapsed, show them how it's done. Follow the diagram. A little practice will make you an expert.

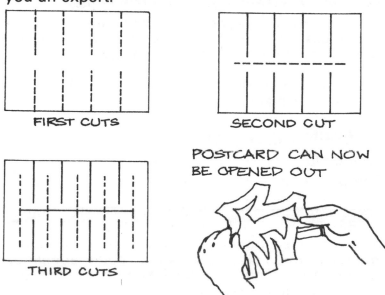

FIRST CUTS

SECOND CUT

THIRD CUTS

POSTCARD CAN NOW BE OPENED OUT

Cut slits about ½" apart beginning with the centre line. Pull postcard gently, folding back all joints in alternate directions.

7 HE CAN DO LITTLE WHO CAN'T DO THIS

You will need a stick.

One of the players takes a poker or stick in his left hand, and transferring it to his right says 'He can do little who can't do this' at the same time knocking the stick three times upon the floor. The other players then must each take the stick in turn and try to imitate him. The trick lies in the stick being taken in the left hand and transferring from thence into the right before knocking it on the floor. The players almost invariably receive the stick in the right hand and transfer it to their left, thereby incurring a forfeit.

8 THE LAST LAUGH

You will need a number of eggs blown, filled with water and resealed, also 2 or 3 raw eggs.

Two demonstrators throw and catch a raw egg, in the process they deliberately smash one. As spectators begin to be amused, start throwing the water filled eggs at them. Make sure your audience is not attired in Sunday best or you may have a big problem on your plate!

9 LIVING CATALOGUE

An idea for a fancy dress party.

The players all come dressed to represent titles of books or poems. For instance, a lady might come dressed to represent T. S. Arthur's 'Tired of Housekeeping'. She could wear an ordinary afternoon dress, with a number of advertisements of 'Board wanted' pinned all over it. A man could appear as 'The Charge of the Light Brigade', his entire suit being covered with gas-bills etc. Endless variations – a prize can be given for the most ingenious.

10 MUMMIES

You will need 2 or 3 toilet rolls.

In pairs the selected players stand back to back. Each pair is then given a toilet roll. On the word 'Go' they try and wrap each other together into a single mummy. The audience volume of applause can judge the winner.

11 PENNY WADDLE

You will need a small bowl, 2p pieces.

A small bowl is placed on the floor. A boy and girl holding hands, each places a penny between their knees and waddle 10 feet and try to drop the penny into the bowl. Played with two small teams it has amusing spectator value.

12 QUAKER'S WEDDING

The one who knows all about it goes round the players and to each person says:

'My friend Obadiah, the son of Zachariah, bids me to inquire of thee if thou wilt go with me to his wedding.'

The answer being 'yes', he must continue:

'Put thy finger to thy lips to keep thyself from laughing, and follow me.'

When all are following, with their fingers to their lips, the leader goes through various movements, which must be imitated by all the others. Finally, he kneels down on one knee, with all close beside him in the same position. When all are quietly kneeling he suddenly leans sideways and the whole group falls to the floor.

13 SMALL BOX STACK

You will need small boxes, about 5 or 6 to each pair.

Couples without using their hands, compete to stack boxes in a vertical column. The team who completes first are the winners.

14 TIGHTROPE TEST

You will need a white tape and a pair of binoculars.

Stretch a white tape across the carpet, and give the performer a pair of binoculars wrong way up, to peer through. Balance is surprisingly difficult. Give the joking onlookers a chance to try for themselves.

15 TOE WRESTLING

Two contestants with bare feet, sit opposite each other and link the big toes. The object is to force the opponent's foot completely over so its side is touching the floor, thus gaining points.